Mr *Wonderful* takes a Cruise

First published in Great Britain in 2004

10 9 8 7 6 5 4 3 2 1

Text © John Nott
Interior illustrations © Ilya
Cover illustrations © Rachel Ross / inkshed.co.uk

John Nott has asserted his right to be identified as the author of
this work under the Copyright, Designs and Patents Act 1988.

First published by
Ebury Press
Random House, 20 Vauxhall Bridge Road, London SW1V 2SA

Random House Australia (Pty) Limited
20 Alfred Street, Milsons Point, Sydney,
New South Wales 2061, Australia

Random House New Zealand Limited
18 Poland Road, Glenfield, Auckland 10, New Zealand

Random House South Africa (Pty) Limited
Endulini, 5A Jubilee Road, Parktown 2193, South Africa

The Random House Group Limited Reg. No. 954009

www.randomhouse.co.uk

A CIP catalogue record for this book
is available from the British Library.

Cover Design by Two Associates
Interior by seagulls

ISBN 009189834X

Printed and bound in UK by Mackays of Chatham

Papers used by Ebury Press are natural, recyclable products
made from wood grown in sustainable forests.

From *When We Were Very Young* © A.A. Milne. Copyright under
the Berne Convention. Published by Methuen, an imprint of
Egmont Books Limited, London and used with permission.

Mr *Wonderful* takes a Cruise

The Adventures of an Old Age Pensioner

John Nott

EBURY
PRESS

This journal covers a series of episodes in the summer of 2002, leading up to a cruise to Norway in October of that year. The characters and incidents in the journal therefore reflect events as they seemed at that time, not as they may appear in the changed circumstances of today.

TO MILOSKA
MY WIFE

for her forbearance
and sense of humour

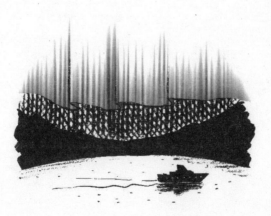

Introduction

I was born before the invention of the pill, television, dishwashers, disposable nappies and New Labour. In those days, a 'chip' was a fried potato. We had 'crumpet' for tea. 'Grass' was mown. 'Coke' was something you put on the fire. A 'joint' was a piece of meat that you ate for Sunday lunch and 'gay' people were the life and soul of the party, not members of the Cabinet.

When I was seven the Second World War began. We were already hungry when food rationing was introduced on 11 March 1940; the coupons we tore out of our ration books entitled us to two eggs, half a packet of butter (4 oz), 4 oz of raw bacon, 12 oz of sugar, etc., every week. My father was away at the war so my Victorian grandfather, a country doctor, presided over the household. He was quite austere and any kind of waste of food or fuel was an abomination to him. Coal was in very short supply so heating was at a premium. Anyone who left a light on in an empty room was in considerable trouble. We had a hot bath once a week and a 3-inch high-water mark was painted around the bath to curb any selfish extravagance. The bath water was not emptied, in accordance with government regulations, so that the fire brigade had a ready supply of water if an incendiary bomb hit the house. Conspicuous consumption existed only among the spivs who had avoided call-up.

Antibiotics were not available and my grandfather had a medicine cupboard with several shelves entirely devoted to a medicine called 'Rhubarb and Soda'. He believed, no doubt correctly, that constipation was the cause of every illness, so that Rhubarb and Soda was prescribed for everything. The entire North Devon community in which we lived was kept alive by my grandfather with liberal doses of Rhubarb and Soda. There was no 'waiting list' as the cure frightened away his patients; it was more upsetting than the illness itself. I don't suppose anyone can yet recognise Great Britain in 2004.

In 1941 I was sent away to boarding school; the food was much improved as the headmaster had useful connections with the local black market. He also hoarded nylon stockings which, given their exceptional rarity, were the guaranteed route to a woman's heart. At school, constipation was once again the enemy, more immediate than the Nazis although the attic was stuffed with packing cases of tinned food in case of an invasion. We were given porridge every morning sprinkled with something new called all-bran.

Boarding school, dominated by the concepts of muscular Christianity, continued until call-up papers for the Army arrived at the age of seventeen. The barrack room consisted of an eclectic mixture of Cockneys, Jocks, Brummies, Mancunians, Geordies, borstal boys and graduates with a heavy leavening of illiterates. Sex was the only unifying force and was virtually the only topic of conversation. I suppose it could be said that I was first in touch with the real world, or *a* real world, at that particular juncture.

I find that sex has *not* gone away. It may have moved out

of the barrack room but, as my journal will confirm, it is now available everywhere, as evidenced by exposed tummy buttons, teenage magazines, in vulgar expletives, in the high street; and in the *Daily Mail* and on Channel 4. It provides a happy link – possibly the only one – with my past.

I regret that something unfortunate happened to me when I left the Army: I had to pursue a career. A man's career is everything. It is absorbing and exclusive, so there was the City, then politics, then business, and there was little opportunity to catch up with the changing world around me. But, at the age of seventy, I found I had *time* on my hands at last. How was I to use it? I had a wife to nurture, a farm to run, a boat to keep me occupied, endless fishing expeditions and country sports but, except for the wife, of course, these were all hobbies, distractions, rather than the obsessions that came with work and a career.

In my seventieth year, I wrote my memoirs, *Here Today, Gone Tomorrow.* The title was not intended to be a statement about human mortality – creeping up on me, I'm afraid – but it was a reference to a phrase used about me by the late Sir Robin Day when I was about to retire from politics. The memoir covered a lifetime of seventy years; this book – the adventures and observations of an old-age pensioner, written in the form of a journal – covers four months in the summer of 2002. I am told that my memoir was irreverent and politically incorrect, so I do not doubt that this book will follow suit and offend the susceptibilities of the young and the political correctness of the liberal élite. That seems a mission worth attempting.

The book is what a journal or diary should be – a series

of apparently disconnected episodes as I set out to discover a new Britain for myself, and how it has changed. I hope at the end of it all to come to some conclusions.

The great thing about being seventy, or maybe eighty, for all I know, is that nothing matters any more. As my writing proceeds, all kinds of memories return, most of them still irreverent, and some of them resurrect themselves in the form of dreams. So this book is a mixture of fact and fiction. My libido troubles me, but mostly it is under reasonable control these days. No great ambition haunts me; money is no problem; creature comforts are sufficient. There is time for contemplation and leisure activity. There are no bawling children; just young grandchildren who come and go.

There are also unexpected pleasures. Instead of all those tiresome sexual urges, I now have a bus pass – a Freedom Pass – an erotic licence of much greater felicity and staying power. It is wonderful to travel every day for free. The 19 and 22 buses from the King's Road to Piccadilly are my new chauffeur-driven carriers. They take me from Chelsea to lunch at my clubs in St James's and Leicester Square. Returning home to Chelsea I always sit upstairs on the port side – there will be much navigational terminology in the following pages – so that I can appreciate the pretty girls among the pavement crowds. Each time we trundle down Knightsbridge I gaze into the shop window of Bradleys were Saudi princes buy underwear for their London tarts. My fellow pensioners should know that Bradleys, La Perla and Agent Provocateur – all famous for their tantalising bras and panties – are all within the radius of a Zimmer frame, and their shop windows are the ultimate aphrodisiac for pensioners like me.

The idea for this journal arose as a result of an advertisement in the *Sunday Telegraph* for a cruise to northern Norway. My wife and I never thought that we would succumb to a cruise, but we did. The episodes recounted in this book lead up to that cruise, they tell of my journeys of discovery around London, my ramblings, and the dreams of a senior citizen – all crammed into a few months. My attendance at 'Mr Wonderful Tea Dances' to brush up my ballroom dancing for that cruise inspired the title of this book.

At the age of forty, many men go through a process of self-examination and frustration about their careers, their lives, their jobs, their marriages. Some women have the impertinence to describe this masculine experience as the 'male menopause'. I can say with confidence that I never suffered from such an affliction in early middle age. At the age of forty I was much too busy for introspection. My career was on the move. But now, by my own choice, I have been voluntarily cast aside or retired. I have no job, no career, no hassle; I simply spend my spare time writing up my journal.

Having decided on this literary adventure, I am prepared to make one concession to modern practice. Nowadays, every government department and business has to flaunt a perfectly meaningless piece of nonsense called a 'mission statement'. I am willing to have one, if only to warn readers of what is to come. I therefore declare my mission statement at the outset. My mission is to grow old disgracefully before the Grim Reaper catches up with me; and if I perplex and upset my children with my eccentric views and unreasonable behaviour, there is nothing that they can do about it. But has the male menopause caught up with me at last? We'll see.

1

Decisions, Decisions, Decisions

'What do you think of this?' I say to my wife. 'The *Sunday Telegraph* is advertising a seven-day cruise up the coast of Norway for an all-inclusive price, including flights from Heathrow, of £950 – that sounds a pretty good bargain to me.'

'What about the ship?' she asks. 'Has it got a Bangladeshi crew with a Greek captain? I don't think I would like that at all – and I wouldn't feel safe with a Greek captain.'

'No,' I reply. 'It is a Norwegian ship with a Norwegian crew and a Norwegian captain. It is known as the Norwegian Coastal Cruise, and it starts in Bergen and then goes up through all the Norwegian fjords, finishing at the Russian border. We then fly back and spend the night in Oslo before returning to Heathrow.'

'When would we go?' she asks.

'We are going fishing in Iceland in early August, then I want to spend the rest of August with the grandchildren at the farm in Cornwall before we go for our usual visit to the South of France in September.'

'How can we fit it all in?'

'Everything turns a bit on the date of the Countryside March,' I say, 'which is on the 22 September. But we can take the last cruise in early October.' So the cruise is booked. A great deal of preparation is needed.

2

'When a man is tired of London he is tired of life'

The driver of the number 19 bus between Chelsea and Piccadilly appears to be both mad and dangerous. He accelerates like crazy and then jams on the brakes. The bus shudders and we are thrown around. The passengers, mainly elderly Indians and Pakistanis, cling on for dear life. At one point the driver even hits the kerb. This is not an unusual occurrence towards the end of the shift when drivers are trying to get home quickly.

On one side of me is a very big, very tall and very ugly Australian girl; across the gangway there is an Irishman and he is drunk, seriously so. The Australian girl starts shouting at the conductor, telling him to get the driver under control. The conductor shouts back: 'Why the f— are you attacking me? I'm not the driver. Anyhow, I don't care.' 'You should care,' replies the Australian girl. 'We are your customers.' 'I don't bloody well care,' repeats the conductor.

The Irishman chips in with his own expletive: 'F— you.' The conductor shouts at the Irishman: 'If you don't

want to f— yourself come on off the bus and *I* will f—
you.' The big Australian girl shouts at the conductor: 'We
are people on this bus, we are customers of yours.' The
conductor shouts back: 'Your type are not my people. I
don't want to have anything to do with people like you. I
would rather shoot myself than have anything to do with
people like you.' At this point the Irishman staggers to his
feet and lunges towards the platform of the bus. The
conductor pulls him back, shouting, 'This is not a stop.'
The Irishman gets aggressive and as the bus slows down at
the traffic lights the conductor decides to push him off.

While this incident is going on, amidst much shouting
and swearing, the Australian girl is firing off at the conductor again: 'Why do you swear all the time? There is such a
thing as politeness on the bus.' The conductor repeats, 'I
don't care. I don't want to work for this effing company
who pays nothing.' At this, overcome with anger and
emotion, he goes up to the Australian girl and thrusts his
body at her: 'Here's my number,' he says, 'write it down.'
'What's your name?' she asks. 'I don't need to effing well
tell you,' shouts the conductor. 'You have my number,
write to the company. I hope they dismiss me.' She replies,
'Then I suppose that you'll go on benefit.' 'You bloody
foreigner,' says the conductor. 'I expect you're on social
security while I'm working.'

By now I have reached my destination and I get off the
bus and say to the conductor, 'Have a nice day.' 'And you,
too,' he replies, in a most courteous tone.

3

'Good manners maketh man
but upset old men'

On the Circle Line, taking the Underground to Westminster, I wonder: has the male menopause caught up with me? On reflection, I think it may have started about ten years ago, when a very polite young man stood up for me on the Northern Line. 'Can I offer you my seat, sir?' he said. The shock was so significant that all I could do was stammer my gratitude and thank him warmly. 'It is very kind of you,' I replied, 'but I am all right.' I was not all right. It was hot, smelly and crowded but I could not admit it . It was really the 'sir' bit that did me in. When young men call me 'sir' I shudder. I know that it is a mark of respect from a well-mannered young person, but it establishes a gulf between us. I don't feel old but clearly the 'sir', wholly well meant, fortifies and makes permanent the fact that he sees me as old and decrepit.

The menopause must have really set in hard when a delightful, pretty girl on the Piccadilly Line did the same thing. This was a catastrophe. 'Do please take my seat, sir,' she said. 'Thank you very much,' I replied, and I accepted. I surrendered to the privilege of old age when I was privately thinking to myself: 'My God! If I was an Arab you'd be young enough to be my third wife.' I looked her up and down, smiling at her all the while, and thought: 'I may be too old for you but you're not too young for me. If I was a multi-millionaire living the social round in New York, I would probably capture you for a young trophy wife.'

One of the things I notice about such courtesies is that whenever a seat is offered me on the bus or on the Underground, it always comes from what I might describe as one of this country's recent immigrants. That first young man may have been born in this country but clearly he was not of English origin. I have never once been offered a seat by a young white man; on the Underground and on the buses it is their loutish behaviour that establishes their crude Anglo-Saxon and Viking heritage; and they share their Viking heritage with me.

4

'I could have danced all night ...'

I have to learn to dance – because ballroom dancing is a mandatory part of every cruise – but finding a dance hall in central London that gives lessons in ballroom techniques proves exceptionally difficult. I search the *Yellow Pages* for old favourites, like the Lyceum Ballroom, which I remember from my youth. But it seems that all these famous places have closed down.

My mother had been keen to prepare her eldest son for life in the fast lane and had taken me on two occasions to visit the Peggy Spencer Dancing Academy in Streatham. Peggy Spencer must be five-score years and thirty by now, but I am sure she is still with us in the spirit, if not in the flesh. Peggy, active in the besequinned gown that she wore for the waltz and a rather short, daring miniskirt for inventions like the tango, grabbed me and whirled me round the dance floor. By this time Peggy Spencer, a world champion, must have been in her forties, and I would guess that she found my sense of timing, balance and Latin looks unsatisfactory. She was always on the lookout for a young partner with whom to win another championship. For me it was an experience of terror mixed with repulsion hence my resistance to attending ballroom dancing ever since.

The *Yellow Pages* do, however, disgorge one possible tea dance, at the Festival Hall, and I am told that only recently the Peggy Spencer demonstration team had laid on a performance there one afternoon. I was also told that the ballroom was full of lady pensioners in miniskirts, wearing fluorescent Lycra and stiletto heels, all demonstrating their athleticism and energy. But this apart, it seems clear that the ancient art of ballroom dancing has given way entirely to other forms of dance – pole dancing or lap dancing, for instance.

I have never been clubbing, as my hearing is already severely damaged (from shooting, not from loud music), and I long ago decided that I could hardly go to a club wearing a pair of ear defenders. These are entirely acceptable on the shooting field, but likely to create comment and surprise in a club or bar. However, to broaden my experience, clubbing I will go.

A lap-dancing establishment, on the other hand, has no dress code. The girls strip off and slide up and down poles of varying kinds. I imagine a seventy-year-old in ear defenders would be neither commented upon nor even noticed. I have been meaning to attend one of the most famous lap-dancing clubs of all, Spearmint Rhino, for some time, but my young friends who are anxious to take me there for a lunchtime session say that at that time of day it is 'rather dark'. I was surprised, because you would imagine that it would be lighter than in the evenings. But, no, I had misunderstood. 'Rather dark' means that the performers are rather dark, and that the white girls come out at night.

So I give up on the *Yellow Pages*. It is a disappointment, because I am a shareholder in the company that bought this famous business.

In a last attempt to find one good ballroom venue, I go on the internet. It is a revelation. The web spawns a mass of venues, mainly in the suburbs, and I know that after a long and fruitless search I have at last hit gold. I look at Malcolm Palmer's famous tea dances at the Secombe Theatre in Cheam Road, Sutton, but the most interesting programme seems to be the offering of 'Mr Wonderful Dancing'. Yes, I could be Mr Wonderful on the dance floor, admired by all. 'Dust off your spoons', 'bring out your harmonica', 'put on your dancing shoes' (I only have studded white-kid golf shoes so I shall have to remove the studs), and 'come to a tea dance' so it says. Tea dances are listed in the British Legion, Edgware; Brent Town Hall; Battersea Town Hall; Chelmsford Assembly Hall; the Irish Centre in Tottenham; the Great Hall in the Bromley Civic Centre; and, on the last Friday of the month, at the Hammersmith Palais.

'Go up Neasden Lane and Blackbird Hill, take the first left into The Paddocks', etc., etc. I am thrilled. I have waited sixty years to go to a tea dance and I am sure that the repulsion caused by the Peggy Spencer Dancing Academy in Streatham can be put behind me for good and all. Of course, I am only going to brush up my technique for the cruise, but I might meet a really delightful pensioner whom I can take in my arms, whispering sweet nothings in her ear, like Bing Crosby or Frank Sinatra dancing with Doris Day.

Norway has no cultural history, or so I hope,
other than a great tradition of plunder, pillage and rape.

5

Culture, English-style?

What further preparations are necessary for this cruise to Norway? I have applied for bridge lessons at the Julian Dobson Bridge Club in Fulham, I am considering taking swimming lessons and my wife is happy that I should subscribe to those dancing lessons with Mr Wonderful. If we were to go on a cruise to the Mediterranean, visiting the sights of ancient Greece and Rome, there would be no problem. On those cruises I believe much of the morning is taken up listening to on-board lectures from junior professors of classical antiquity from polytechnics – sorry, universities – in the North of England. However, Norway has no cultural history, or so I hope, other than a great tradition of plunder, pillage and rape. I suppose that if the United States is full of museums displaying the ancient history of America, Norway will also be able to muster up some museums boasting of its great cultural past. We shall see.

I cannot be sure, but I believe that my ancestors are of Viking stock. Certainly my name is derived from Old Norse, the Scandinavian Knott, Cnut, Kuut, Canute, etc., so on the cruise to Norway I will be able to test the validity of my

DNA. What I am hoping to find is that my Viking ancestors were entirely devoid of culture, but I have no doubt
that, in spite of this, I shall be told of the long cultural
history of the north Norwegian Vikings and their Eskimo
neighbours, just as I have been told how the desert Arabs
invented algebra, how Shakespeare came from Nigeria and
that Jesus was a woman.

The truth of the matter is that I positively shudder at
the word 'culture', and in particular at the notion of
cultural subsidies to the arts. In that I conform to a good
Tory stereotype. I can say that I have spent far too many
boring and useless hours at Covent Garden and at the
National Theatre in an endeavour to improve my cultural
credentials. In fact, my concept of true English culture is
not sitting listening to Beethoven in the Albert Hall or
going to *The Barber of Seville* at the Coliseum but sitting
around a blazing fire in a country house with a wet spaniel
beside me on the sofa. Why anyone should prefer to follow
metropolitan pursuits when you can be on a steaming
horse in the pouring rain chasing after a half-drowned fox
is beyond me. Culture for me exists in the village pub, not
sitting in a subsidised provincial opera house listening to
some fat blonde wheezing her way through an aria.

6

Viagra: Life after Death

As part of my attempt to understand modern Britain, I note that when young men are in their cups (intoxicated) they make ribald jokes about old men and Viagra. One of them had the impertinence to ask me recently whether I suffered from creaking bones and stiffening limbs – only one stiffening limb would be welcome to you now, he joked, ha! ha! – and that is available not from the Almighty's corporate representative on earth, the Pope, but from Pfizer, the manufacturers of Viagra.

The young man made me feel old and out of touch, because I had never sampled this modern wonder drug. I really must get 'with it'. So I set off nervously to my doctor in Sloane Street to obtain a prescription for Viagra. 'You are not eligible,' he says, 'to obtain Viagra under the NHS.' I protest. 'As an old-age pensioner,' I say, 'I am eligible for a free bus pass; why am I not eligible for free Viagra? I can afford a bus ticket but assuredly I cannot afford Viagra at £6 per pill.' 'You do not conform,' he repeats, 'to the category of essential users set down by Mr Blair.'

The doctor takes my blood pressure several times and is clearly confronted by a medical dilemma. 'I can give you a prescription,' he says, 'but I advise you not to use it for non-marital couplings. If you find,' he adds, 'that you have not reverted to a "natural state" after four hours you should call a doctor.' 'Four hours,' I say. 'My God! Would the doctor in these circumstances make a rare home visit in such an emergency?' I ask. 'For it would be highly embarrassing for a member of Her Majesty's Most Honourable Privy Council to walk to the surgery down Sloane Street in an engorged state.' Although, I think to myself, there are thousands of members of the Metropolitan Police comfortably filling out forms in police stations throughout the capital, it would be just my luck to be arrested by the only policeman actually patrolling the streets of London on this occasion.

In the South of France, in contrast to London, one sees a handsome young policeman on every street corner. Indeed, to keep the ladies happy many of them put on plastic pants and bicycle around the streets showing off their handsome calves and tight little bottoms. If they were to see an old-age pensioner from England wandering down the street in Nice in an engorged state they would cheer: '*Ah, mon vieux, vous êtes Anglais – superbe, mon vieux. Bonne chance, monsieur!*' In England one would land up in Pentonville, sentenced for indecent exposure by a New Labour magistrate appointed by Mr Blair's erstwhile patron, the infamous Lord Irvine. In France a seventy-year-old man like me would be awarded the Légion d'Honneur for parading his manhood in a public place.

7

Introduction to the Tea Dance

Off to Bromley to reconnoitre my first Mr Wonderful tea dance. The first surprise is how close Bromley is to London Victoria. I had left my bus pass – my Freedom Pass – at home, so instead of a free trip the Underground costs me a scandalous £3.60 for a return ticket from Sloane Square to Victoria, and another £2.60 to travel to Bromley South and back. On arrival in Bromley I decide to have some lunch and go into the Slug & Lettuce where I am served by a really lovely young waitress, helpful, quick and cheerful. After lunch I set off to find the Great Hall in the Bromley Civic Centre.

Mr Wonderful in Bromley. What can I say to reproduce the sense of nostalgia which the first sight of the dance hall brings back to me? It is like one of those films of the Second World War where off-duty airmen dance in a dimly lit village hall during the blackout with an assorted group of pretty blondes played by Dinah Sheridan and Greer Garson. It is all in black and white. Respectable, contained and innocent, but these same blondes of the 1940s have grown up into forty or so grey-haired lovelies still wearing the same cotton-print dresses of their youth. Somehow it seems that nothing very much has changed them in the intervening fifty years. You can see that they have been pretty, for the majority have quite good features; it's true that they appear to be rather more wary – life has made them more cautious – but there is still a sparkle in their eyes. Here they are with Mr Wonderful in Bromley and they are going to enjoy their afternoon.

After paying my £2.50 entrance fee I slip away to the Gents, or the toilets as Mr Wonderful would call them. I had smartened myself up by putting on a jacket and tie but some of the performers are in short-sleeved nylon shirts – so I remove my jacket to watch. The atmosphere is great – cheerful, friendly and happy. There is an equal balance between women and men and the elderly ladies sitting around the hall are quite quickly snapped up by male part- ners. I watch the cha-cha-cha, the rumba, samba, waltz and the slow foxtrot and as I watch I realise that the dancing is very professional; there is no way that I can possibly take the floor. I would make a complete fool of myself (they say that dancing is ritual humiliation in pursuit of sex). Instead, I chat to any lady or gentleman that I can find.

Most of the participants seem to live in Greater London and travel around to attend these dances. I am told that the Brent Town Hall dances are rough, Battersea Town Hall is lovely, the Covent Garden Opera House is really great with a real dance band culled from the Opera House orchestra. Although all the participants are very competent and know their steps well, the most professional is a peroxide blonde. I would say she is much younger than the average; I would have put her at sixty-five. She is snapped up quickly in turn by every man in the hall. She is wearing a purple dress with a long flared skirt – bought at Etam, I would guess – and she seems to have an accent, Polish, possibly. She is definitely the glamour girl of Mr Wonderful in Bromley. The DJ who switches on and off the gramophone is a charming middle-aged Indian who dashes between the recording equipment and the closest female victim. He certainly charms all the ladies.

As I sit out the dances, I talk to the lady nearest to me. She says she follows Mr Wonderful around and shows great loyalty to these dances. She lives in Finchley and I find her very well informed and intelligent. She lends me her copy of the *Dance Diary* – the encyclopaedia of future events: 'More than four times more foxtrots than any other publication.'

At three o'clock there is a break for tea and a collective dash by eighty or so pensioners for the service hatch. I have a cup of tea and a KitKat costing me 70p – good value. Looking around at the men, they are mostly bald: an assorted clutch of retired bank clerks, plumbers, civil servants and merchant navy retired. Quite ordinary but decent folk, it seems, who have seen it all and are now free from the drudgery of work, commuting in dirty trains, bringing up families and struggling to pay the bills but having saved, saved, saved for a fun old age: ballroom dancing, cruises, summers in Spain. It has taken fifty years to gain their freedom. At last they are released from the nine-to-five, and seem to be fit and healthy enough still to enjoy their independence, beholden to no one any more except themselves.

At the tea break I sit at a plastic table in the civic centre's canteen. 'Tell me,' I ask the rather distinguished looking couple at my table, 'do you come here often? I mean, do you go around to all these Mr Wonderful dancing sessions?' 'Oh, yes,' she says, 'we live in Dartford but we always try and attend these tea dances, especially in the autumn.' I make a mental note to visit Dartford. 'I think it's Brent Town Hall next week and the Hammersmith Palais in a fortnight's time.' 'What else do you do in retirement?' I ask. 'Next week,' she says, 'we are going on a cruise to the Canaries to celebrate Bill's eightieth birthday.' 'You don't look eighty,' I reply. 'No,' he laughs, 'Betty keeps me young. We have only been married for three years. We were both widowed, you see. Betty was alone for seven years but I was only a widower for three. We got together and we enjoy life.' Trying to keep conversation going, I say that my wife had treated me to a seventieth birthday party in Madeira. Bill and Betty feel Madeira is slightly overrated now that it has become a tourist destination.

'We love our cruises,' says Bill. 'We have done the Nile, the Caribbean and the Mediterranean – all great fun, but nothing compares to the Alaska cruise. That's the best.'

I can see that Betty had been something of a glamour girl in her youth. She has neatly cut grey hair, fine features and quite intelligent, piercing eyes. Actually she is rather sexy. I ponder on whether I would choose a restless, naked blonde squirming around a pole in Spearmint Rhino or this more experienced woman of the world. It would be difficult. Applying the wisdom of Solomon, I decide that the ideal would be a threesome, but if I was forced to make a choice I would go for ten minutes with the pole dancer but a whole night of comfort, whispered confidences and slow, warm embraces with Betty. Yes, Betty would win the race every time.

I decide after tea that I have had enough of Mr Wonderful, so I set off around the town. As part of my investigation I decide to call at Ann Summers in the High Street, that great emporium to culture, taste and leisure in modern Britain. At the front of the shop it is all skimpy bras and knickers but at the back, reserved for adults, there are four or five teenage girls on a reconnaissance. As I get to the back of the shop they are examining the vibrators in their various shapes and sizes and discussing the multiplicity of functions that these machines perform. They talk in slightly hushed but unembarrassed tones as to which particular dildo most catches their fancy. Involved as I am in serious academic research, I want to give them some advice, but it would be inappropriate.

I have indeed read, in an interview with Jacqueline Gold, the managing director of Ann Summers and often in the running for Businesswoman of the Year, that they have sold nearly one million units of the Rampant Rabbit. 'It's amazing, it rotates, it vibrates, it stimulates and it's multi-speed.' Some wag had added that on request it even came with a rabbit hutch and lettuce. However, I would clearly be subject to a charge of sexual abuse of minors if I should even glance at these girls, so I discreetly absent myself. As I leave I see that one of them has broken off from her comrades-in-arms and is purchasing two pairs of briefs on each of which is inscribed the useful advice: 'Please me, tease me' and 'Ripe and ready'.

As I leave the shop it occurs to me that these young women are clearly more prepared for their wedding night – or what passes for a similar experience – by their knowledge and handling of these monstrous rubber and plastic mechanical toys than their Victorian great-grandmothers could ever have been. But there is a serious problem. Whereas the Victorian bride was, by all accounts, horrified at what she discovered on her wedding night, these modern young women are more likely to be horrified by the relatively minor proportions of the real thing when they compare it with the huge mechanical dildos on display at Ann Summers.

Since I am on this distasteful subject, perhaps this is the place to tell the story of an old friend of similar age who visited an Ann Summers superstore somewhere in the southern counties. In a hushed and embarrassed tone he asked the attractive girl behind the counter whether he could purchase a 'Humming-bird' for his wife. 'Oh no!' said the young lady. 'The humming-bird was superseded many years ago. It was made of seven inches of hard plastic; we now use Aryan flesh-coloured latex. We are more knowledgeable, more adventurous, today,' she said.

'Well,' said my friend. 'In that case, could you recommend a vibrator for my wife?' 'Of course,' said the young lady. 'We have a very wide range, but I especially recommend one here. We call it the "Camilla". It is much favoured by the British aristocracy. If you would like a special presentation version of the Camilla we sell it, in a limited edition, in a wooden box lined with ermine and some of our customers particularly like the inscription on the box which reads: "*Honi soit qui mal y pense*".'

Only a few yards from Ann Summers is the local Etam branch. I was chairman of Etam some ten years ago. As I enter the Etam shop to examine the clothes I am greatly flattered when the manageress comes up to me and recognises me; we talk about old times. She tells me that she has worked for Etam for thirty years and even remembers a visit I made to the Lewisham store. We discuss the hugely entertaining atmosphere at our in-house fashion shows in those days, when we called in some two hundred manageresses from all around the United Kingdom with an average age of around thirty; the bawdy humour, the cheers and titters as the models swayed down the catwalk is a memory to be savoured.

I was asked to take the chairmanship of Etam just after it had fought off a takeover bid by some South Africans. I enjoyed the stores and the people; it was the best job I ever had. I imagine that my City experience was thought appropriate for the job, but I knew absolutely nothing about women's fashions so, when I went around the stores, I put on a knowledgeable air, handled the garments professionally and admired the layout of the clothes; it fooled no one. My only knowledge of women's clothes had been garnered as a teenager, when I had failed repeatedly to remove girls' bras – the most daring thing we did in those far-off days. I used to fumble with the clasp and never ever did it come apart.

The point of this apparently irrelevant observation is merely to record that when I was thrown out of this important assignment – i.e. discharged as chairman – the former chief executive of Etam approached me to invest in a newly formed lingerie company called Agent Provocateur. I took my chauffeur on a secret mission to Soho to suss out this establishment and, pulling my hat low over my face, I entered the shop. There were two good-looking, half-dressed shop assistants who welcomed me warmly. They were quite used to men of my generation shopping for their mistresses and buying see-through nighties and the rest to encourage not the mistress but the *demandeur*. I was shown an array of really delightful garments and noted them down for future occasions.

I consulted two of my children – my daughter, who had a degree in fashion from St Martin's School of Art, and my younger son, who hadn't – about the sponsors, and discovered from him that one of them was the son of Vivienne Westwood and Malcolm McLaren, the former manager of the Sex Pistols. Now Vivienne Westwood is a genius. I have sat in numerous catwalk shows as a distinguished member of the rag trade and, although her clothes are clearly not meant to be worn by any normal person, they disclose an imaginative genius, no less. I did not invest in Agent Provocateur, given that my son in particular advised me against it, and I considered him an expert from the time that he worked in a shop called The Duffer of St George, also in Soho. But nowadays, having been the successful purveyor of underwear to a series of performers from Madonna down, Agent Provocateur has set up shop in Pont Street. There, standing in the window, are three thin, sexy mannequins clothed in fishnet stockings and underwear. This is directly on the route to my doctor in Sloane Street. Had I known this, my Viagra visit would have proved unnecessary.

Last Christmas, as is my custom, I left my Christmas shopping very late and happened to pass by La Perla in Sloane Street, then Bradleys in Knightsbridge, and finally Agent Provocateur in Pont Street. Each of the items on display was hugely pricey but in La Perla and Agent Provocateur I managed, as a joke of course, to purchase a frilly thong for each of the younger female members of my family. I am not sure that they saw the joke but they laughed indulgently. In Bradleys I found a nightie for my wife which would gladden the eye of a Saudi prince. Unfortunately, desperate to catch my train from Paddington, I also grabbed the first item on the counter – a pair of black fishnet stockings with a thin black seam. I was excited by my Christmas present but all my wife said when I gave it to her was: 'How stupid. How can I wear fishnet stockings? I am sixty-seven.' So much for marriage.

8

The Survey

The doorbell rings in Chelsea, and I answer it to a woman with a clipboard in her hand. 'I am sorry to trouble you,' she says, 'but we are conducting a survey. Would you mind if I took up a few minutes of your time?' I like the look of her so I invite her in.

As we mount the stairs to the sitting room, I am thinking to myself that this is a great opportunity; she is obviously doing a survey for a deodorant manufacturer, or, better still, for a political 'focus group', and it has long been an ambition of mine to f— up a focus group, and ensure that Mr Philip Gould or whoever gets a completely distorted view of my true opinion. In this way it is possible to ruin a whole raft of government policies. Politics is conducted these days on the basis of what people answer to a list of inane one-liners that cannot sensibly be reduced to a single yes or no answer. 'Answer the question, is it yes or no?' Worse still, you have to tick a box or claim that you have no opinion.

For instance: 'please tick one of the following boxes'. The question is: 'Do you like sex?' 'Very much – much – a little – sometimes – once a year – never – or, I have no opinion.' The real answer is, of course, 'very much' or 'never', depending on one's mood or whether the wife was nice to you at breakfast. But most people tick the box 'much' because it is impossible to reduce such a complex issue of human behaviour to a single answer. Because the answer is 'much', the opinion pollster reports that the interviewee likes it 'once a week'.

So when the lady is comfortably settled on my sofa she begins: 'This survey is absolutely confidential – and if you wish to say nothing we will respect your privacy,' etc., etc.

'First, I need to place you in one of our social categories – I am sure you will understand: are you an "A" (higher managerial or professional – Chief Constable, barrister, etc.), a "B" (intermediate managerial – air-traffic controller, parson, squadron leader in the RAF, etc.), a "C1" (supervisory – bank cashier, RSPCA inspector, etc.), a "C2" (skilled manual worker – barber, bus driver, etc.), a "D" (semi-skilled manual worker, window cleaner, fork-lift truck driver, minicab driver, etc.) or "E" (state pensioner, unemployed for more than six months, widow, etc.)?'

'That is easy,' I reply. 'I am definitely an "E". I am a state pensioner.'

'No,' she says, rather irritated, I think. 'That is for our analysts to decide. In any event, we do not call people like you "pensioners"; we address you as "senior citizens."'

'Sorry,' I say. 'What are your questions?'

She begins. Question one: 'Your age profile. Are you nearer sixteen – twenty – fifty – or ninety?'

Question two: 'Do you consider yourself to be "working class" – "middle class" – "upper class" – "an aristocrat" – or "a minor royal"?'

Question three: 'Do you consider yourself to be "black" – "white" – "coffee" – or "yellow"?'

She looks at me enquiringly. Surely she can see the answer, I think, but I answer: 'I am sixteen, black and I consider myself to be a minor royal.'

'That's most interesting,' she says. 'We haven't had one of those before.'

Bearing in mind that I am now slotted into a particular social category for electoral or consumption purposes, I keep up the good work. The lady smiles sweetly and asks me the next question: 'Which political party do you support: Labour – New Labour – Liberal – Liberal Democrat – British National Party – UK Independence Party – Monster Raving Loony Party?'

The true answer is, of course, 'Conservative', but as I haven't been asked the question I answer 'the Monster Raving Loony Party', hence the survey conclusion that the Conservatives will never be returned at the next general election.

'So, you are sixteen years of age, black, a direct descendant of Queen Victoria, and you support the Monster Raving Loony Party at elections. Is that correct?' she asks.

'Yes,' I say, 'that is correct.'

'I have to ask you next,' she says, 'about your daily consumption of alcohol.' (Guinness is contributing to the cost of the survey.) 'Do you drink daily: 15 cans of lager – 3 bottles of Château Latour – 9 bottles of Tesco White –

a glass of Ribena or Westminster Still Mineral Water (Thames recycled sewage) – or none of these?'

I hesitate because the real answer is 'none of these'. But it depends. If I am feeling good (unlikely), I drain an entire bottle of Château Mouton-Rothschild '82 (cost £650) or on other days I have a glass of Asda Red (cost 60p). But if I answer 'none of these' it would imply that I don't drink, which would be untrue. So I opt for the 'Tesco White'. This revelation is duly returned to Tesco, who are so encouraged by this marketing intelligence that they decide to build a complex of new stores with white wine bays, like their Calais warehouse (cost £30 million).

'That is very interesting. You are a sixteen-year-old, black, minor royal, who has sex once a week and you drink half a bottle of Tesco White each day. Is that correct?' she says.

'Yes, that's quite correct,' I reply.

'Finally,' she says, 'I must ask you about your diet.' (Sainsbury's is contributing to the cost of the survey.) 'I have to tick one of the following boxes,' she says. 'If you have breakfast, can you say which of these most approximates to your normal diet? Bacon, 3 eggs, 4 sausages, baked beans, grilled tomatoes, mushrooms, black pudding (the full English breakfast) – or do you have a cup of lemon tea, a slice of wheat bread, grapefruit slices, some Dutch cheese, and a yoghurt (the Savoy breakfast) – or neither of these?'

The correct answer is neither of these, because it depends on where I am staying and the state of the weather. So I say 'neither of these'.

The good lady protests: 'Surely you have some breakfast?'

'Yes,' I say, rather embarrassed, 'I have a bowl of All Bran each morning.'

'All Bran,' she says. 'How very interesting. I will make a special note on the survey. (Kellogg's may be persuaded to contribute to the next survey.)

'Well,' says the lady, 'thank you very much. It has been a valuable set of answers. You are sixteen years old, black, a minor royal, who has sex once a week, drinks a glass of Tesco White each evening and has All Bran for breakfast.'

She ticks the box 'Social Category E', which is what I said all along. He is obviously New Labour, she reports, although he says he is a Loony. Mr Blair will be ecstatic when he next meets Mr Philip Gould, who will assure him that the 'Es', the underclass (state pensioners, etc.) are moving back to New Labour.

9

Bridge Lessons in Fulham

I set off on the 22 bus for the Julian Dobson Bridge Club in Parson's Green, Fulham, a famous establishment formerly situated above Boots in the King's Road. Sitting beside me on the bus is a very pretty girl wearing boots, a very short skirt which just about covers her pubic area and a T-shirt on which is emblazoned in huge black letters the slogan: *Utter Contempt for Tradition.* I tell her that I like her slogan, her sartorial taste, and that I share her anarchist instincts; we get into a conversation. She is a student at the Chelsea College of Art and, in about fifteen minutes, we exchange a host of experiences about life and information about each other. I decide – vanity, of course – that I am very good at chatting up pretty girls and as I appear to be approaching eighty and am very relaxed, they do not see me as a threat. Ah, the naïvety of youth.

I have registered for a weekend Beginners' Class, starting at 10 a.m. on Saturday, as it is quite certain that I shall need bridge for the cruise. There are many famous bridge players – the Marx Brothers, President Dwight D. Eisenhower, Elizabeth Taylor, Kojak, Livshitz (the Russian

Champion in 1990) – but my hero is Omar Sharif, playing captain of the Egyptian team at the World Team Olympics, 1968. If I grow a black moustache, put Grecian 2000 on my hair, like Ronald Reagan, pull my shoulders back and use Maclean's Whitener on my teeth, I may well be mistaken for Omar at the bridge table.

While I am waiting to register for the weekend course, I browse through the one thousand pages of *The Official Encyclopaedia of Bridge*. I don't get much beyond the As, but I learn about the 'Alternative Squeeze' (there is also a Backwash and Vice Squeeze), the 'Alcatraz Coup', the 'Alligator Coup', 'Absolute Force', 'Active Ethics', (Ha! Ha!), 'Advanced Lebensohl' and 'Aspro' (a method of defending against a no-trumps opening bid).

After getting a cup of coffee from Graznya, a young Polish girl, I look around the room at my fellow students. I notice that most of the men look like retired colonels and they all have a little moustache like Omar Sharif or Adolf Hitler. Is a moustache a necessary attribute for champion-ship bridge? I had been told that the club is patronised by a galaxy of elderly female Sloanes, all looking for a partner – and not just for bridge. As an Omar Sharif lookalike, the prospects of 'pulling' an elderly Sloane are good.

The encyclopaedia tells me about the Bennet murder in Kansas City in 1932, the year of my birth. John Bennet, a prosperous perfumer, met his death at the hands of his wife when she became so infuriated at her husband's play that she pulled the family revolver from a drawer and shot him dead. I realise that bridge is a very dangerous game. The judge in this case was a bridge player himself and he understood; she was acquitted. I learn that the choice of partner is very important – and it is probably wise not to choose a divorcée Sloane, as they can be violent.

But alas, across the room I spy a representative of that nearly extinct and endangered species: a Tory MP. He is accompanied by a very tall wife. He is rather tiny but 'perfectly formed', as *Private Eye* would say. We greet each other like long-lost friends meeting in an unwelcome world, although we hardly know one another. I select a likely looking lady as my partner but I cannot help noticing that most of the women seem to be wearing standard-issue kit – a Gucci scarf and handbag (artificial, bought in Hong Kong), blue skirts, blue blouses, blue jackets and comfortable flat shoes. I decide that this is where the defeated Tories have retreated to bring up supplies, regroup and regain their strength before the counterattack on the vandals of New Labour. Bridge clubs and Women's Institutes all over the country are the chosen assembly point for the counterrevolution.

The teaching begins and I learn about bidding, scoring, a balanced hand, finding fits, responding when the opener is balanced, responding to suit openers, making tricks in no trumps, overcalling, etc., etc. The whole thing is perfectly frightening. It is a long time since I went through an educational process. I always hated education of any kind. Education goes on the whole weekend. I discover that I am far and away the dimmest of our bridge four and my attention span is very limited. The MP's tall wife is, intellectually, especially daunting, but deliciously appealing; and her husband is a man of considerable personality and humour.

Throughout the weekend my concentration is tested beyond endurance. Nonetheless, if I apply a heavy dose of gamesmanship (better known as bullshit in military circles), look confident at all times, refuse to be fooled by 'Little Old Ladies' (an expression in bridge describing an apparently innocent player who unexpectedly bids and plays against you as though they are a world champion), reject intimidation by other bullshitters and cheat wherever necessary, I may be qualified to join bridge evenings on the cruise.

10

Tea Dance in Battersea

I decide to attend the second of my tea dances organised by Mr Wonderful, this time in Battersea Town Hall. I set off on the 345 bus, alighting in Clapham Junction and walking up Lavender Hill. The bus is mainly occupied by a whole army of mommas and as we go along, an increasing number of pushchairs are manhandled on to the bus, with some of the youngsters yowling and bawling in their prams. It is not a peaceful journey. I am very courteously directed to the Town Hall. I find a rather interesting but slightly run-down building and am shown to the ballroom around the side. I pay my £3 entrance (50p more than Bromley) and wander into the hall.

The atmosphere is tremendous, really happy and lively. I just sit there in wonder that such events still take place. I am genuinely transfixed by the atmosphere. The man sitting next to me says that Battersea Town Hall is the best venue of the lot; it is clean and well decorated. Indeed it is. There is a new dance floor and a rather exceptional deco-rated ceiling.

But it is the people who take my fancy. There is a large

Chinese contingent and the Chinese ladies, most of them in late middle age, provide a considerable dash of glamour. They are very well dressed and one particular lady has a sort of muslin skirt showing off the best pair of legs that I have seen for many a time. The European contingent does not really compete in the glamour stakes, as they are rather overweight and generally have heavy bodies, but they move quite lightly across the dance floor and without exception they know the steps. When the waltz comes along, Mr Wonderful in person, my Indian friend from Bromley, keeps on announcing 'change your partners, change your partners' and I, a wallflower hiding against the wall, am repeatedly propositioned by a succession of beautiful Chinese, European and Indian ladies who try to drag me on to the floor. Covered in embarrassment I tell them that I cannot dance, which in retrospect is ridiculous because, after all, I am here to brush up my ballroom techniques for the forthcoming cruise.

I cannot help noticing the two best-dressed men in the hall. They are both black and they wear very black suits and very black shirts with startling white ties. They seem to fit in without any apparent hesitation with a succession of Chinese and European female dancing partners. I only notice these rather immaculately turned-out figures only because their Anglo-Saxon counterparts, almost without exception, are in the ubiquitous short-sleeved nylon shirt and tie. There is a Chelsea Pensioner who has taken off his jacket but I recognise his trousers, blue shirt, Army belt and tie. I really want to plunge in and become part of it all but I am too shy to do so.

I pick up the future programme, which includes the Hammersmith Palais, which I shall attend shortly. There is also a New Year dance weekend at the Fort Lodge Hotel in Margate. Three whole days of dancing, including a black tie gala dinner, tea dances, full English breakfasts and rooms with double beds. Three days of dancing, eating and accommodation are offered at a cost of £89 per person. Pretty good, I think. Why don't I want to attend a three-day dancing orgy in Margate? Bernard Shaw observed that 'dancing is a perpendicular expression of a horizontal desire'. Maybe that is what the Margate weekend is all about, but I doubt it. Mr Wonderful just seems like innocent fun among the elderly.

I have a cup of tea and biscuits (free) and a whole bevy of prospective dancing partners smile sweetly at me. It is the smiles and the friendliness that is the most marked part of the Mr Wonderful at the Battersea Town Hall.

Wandering back to Clapham Junction, I see that the school children are on their way home. Nearly every child is black. These children are now all fully-fledged and integrated British citizens. They were all born here, like me, and are as much part of modern Britain as an old pensioner like myself.

I am reminded of Daniel Defoe's poem on 'The True-Born Englishman':

There are Heroes who despite the Dutch,
And rail at new-come Foreigners so much;
Forgetting that themselves are all deriv'd
From the most Scoundrel race that ever liv'd.

A horrid Crowd of Rambling Thieves and Drones,
Who ransacked Kingdoms and dispeopled Towns:
The Pict and Painted Briton, Treach'rous Scot
By Hunger, Theft and Rapine hither brought,
Norwegian Pirates, Buccaneering Danes,
Whose Red-haired Offspring everywhere remains;
Who joined with Norman-French compound the Breed
From whence your True-Born Englishmen proceed.

With apologies to Daniel Defoe, I add:

In huge numbers the Invading Hordes arrive,
The Cry goes up from True-Born Englishmen –
     We Must Survive.
Jamaicans, Afghans, Indians, Pakistanis too,
The former subjects of an Empire we must woo.
For they as much as us, have much to Share
As preaches Mighty Monarch Mr Blair.
We are a polyglot Nation in a Hurry,
Fuelled by a diet of Naan and Curry.

My visit to Lavender Hill for the Mr Wonderful Tea Dance whets my appetite to discover other areas of London where I can see the New Britain going about its business. I saw few white faces in Clapham Junction. I wonder how it will compare with other parts of London.

11

Matins at the Royal Hospital

I fear that in this country, except among Muslim newcomers, Mammon has ousted God. It was not always so. The spiritual side of life in modern Britain is of interest to me, although my journal concentrates on life temporal – very temporal, I have to say. Nonetheless I decide to examine two aspects of religion in Britain today, the traditional and the modern.

First, matins in the Wren Chapel at the Royal Hospital, Chelsea. A few Pensioners are present, looking splendid in their red coats and medals. How wonderful it is that there is somewhere where old soldiers can spend their last few years in comradeship and dignity. I think that the Wren dining hall beside the chapel is the finest in all of London, smaller but equal to the painted hall at Greenwich and Hampton Court.

The service taken by our admirable chaplain is a fine traditional English matins, which hardly exists any more in the Church of England. Now, in most parishes, we are all afflicted with family communion, happy-clappy priests and readings from that illiterate abomination The New English

Bible – and all the while the Anglican church is declining. Here at least I can attend a short ceremony in wonderful surroundings with one of the most splendid choirs in London; they make me weep, as do the Nunc Dimittis and the 121st Psalm. 'I will lift up mine eyes unto the hills, from whence cometh my help. My help cometh even from the Lord, who hath made heaven and earth.' Great, great poetry. It can all be a great spiritual experience.

The service begins and the choir sings the introit in the lobby of the chapel. It is quite beautiful and moving. The chapel is full; many of the visitors are Americans who no doubt find the order of service a little strange. I do not doubt that the self-confidence, the evangelical desire to convert, to propagate the gospel of democracy to the world, even the arrogance of power among Americans, greatly stems from the widespread religious convictions of the American people. Religion and the arrogance of power seem to go together in the American religious right. They believe that they can conquer the world with the power of their ideas. Karl Marx believed the same. It is all rather different from the Christian teaching of humility.

Evensong at Holy Trinity, Brompton

The average age of the congregation at the Royal Hospital I would put at sixty-five, so as part of my curiosity about the changing spiritual side of life in modern Britain I decide that I must visit Holy Trinity, Brompton, a birthplace in England of charismatic evangelism; here I am told that the average age of the congregation is nearer twenty-five.

The chaplain of the Royal Hospital is polite about HTB, as they call themselves, but implies that it makes life, or religion, all too simple; there are no shades of grey. At one extreme, he says, ritual takes over with smells and bells and at the other it is all about emotion and scripture, with no room for tradition. He thinks that religion is a three-legged stool – scripture, tradition and reason – and they need to be in balance. I like his moderation.

When I arrive at Holy Trinity for an evening prayer gathering at 7 p.m. the place is packed to the roof with several hundred young people in jeans, trainers and sweat-shirts. There are some older people, too. The atmosphere is akin to a rather upmarket pop concert. One of the many

ordained parsons of HTB asks us all to stand and a huge
screen is lit up with a succession of hymns and songs:

> 'Breathe on me breath of God'
> 'I'm desperate for you (Lord)
> And I'm lost without you'
> etc.

The band is excellent – three electric guitars and an electronic organ, with two pretty young girl singers leading a
succession of rather beautiful and soft hymns as the words
change on the screen. The congregation sings along with
real joy – it is pure religious karaoke – and many sway with
the music and hold their hands high. Uninhibited, personal
and really very moving. The girls in the huge congregation
seem particularly affected with this revivalism – and I can
see that this religious movement has changed their lives.

The singing goes on too long for my old legs so I sit
down, but then a young girl steps forward and reads her
own prayer: 'Thank you, Lord, for our freedom. Let us
pray for Mr Blair, the Queen [in that order], the NHS,
Israel, Iraq, the Congo and Zimbabwe.'

There is a reading of the Bible (John 7: 37) by another
young person: 'Let anyone who is thirsty come to me and
drink. Who ever believes in me will have streams of living
water flowing from within.'

This is the text of the sermon by Nicky Gumbel who,
with Sandy Millar, is the leading inspiration of this revival.
He is immaculately dressed in jeans and a white, white shirt
and he is lit by a spotlight. He is smooth, grey-haired and

a little too much of a media star for my taste – there is a bit of vanity there somewhere. But no one can deny his professionalism – or should I say his political arts? He reminds me of another former barrister, Mr Tony Blair.

I leave very puzzled by it all – it is the ultimate happy-clappy occasion but I am tremendously impressed. This is the most interesting and important of all my enquiries. If the traditional Church of England is declining, this movement is growing like an amoeba. Over a generation it could change the spiritual life of our country.

I decide that I have had enough of all this masochistic activity
so I return to the locker room under two notices saying
'One life live it well' and 'Have faith in your body'.

13

Holmes Place

My wife is out and it is pouring with rain outside. I can't stand the television and I can't sit at home all day, so I decide to make a rare visit to Holmes Place, my health club in the Fulham Road. As I enter the club I hear the 'thump, thump, thump' of aerobics on an upper floor. So, out of curiosity, I climb the stairs to peep. There is a very large and very muscular black instructor, stripped to the waist with a microphone strapped to his head, leading twelve or so nubile women in 'body combat' aerobics. They are sweating profusely in their designer pants and vests. As they aim right hooks and straight lefts at an imaginary punch bag, I wonder if they are training to take on Mike Tyson, or maybe just their lovers.

Actually, no, they are indulging in a bout of body-building, part of the gym culture of today. I asked my daughter-in-law to explain to me why young women indulge in this activity, and she replied: 'It's all to do with sex and status. If you're looking good, you're bound to get a good job, and get laid.'

When I was young, outside of school and boxing gyms

in the East End of London, there were no gyms. Exercise was taken in compulsory sports at school and even the most weedy, sickening, spotty youth was forced into the school boxing competition and endless cross-country runs. Cold baths every freezing winter morning were an advanced form of torture, and the idea of anyone voluntarily taking a cold shower to tone up the body would have seemed absurd.

Anyhow, I dress up from my locker in the standard uniform and enter the mixed gym; young men and women, simply covered in sweat, torture themselves on bicycle and running machines, watching Sky Sports on the television in front of them as they do so. The women, I notice, concentrate on arm and chest machines for bust development and leg racks for tightening the thigh muscles. There is an old man of around my age being twisted into unnatural shapes by his personal instructor. I decide that I have had enough of all this masochistic activity, so I descend the stairs to the locker room under the beaming eye of a notice saying 'One Life, Live It Well' and another exhorting 'Have Faith in Your Body'. I decide these fitness fanatics are demented; they will all go home to watch *Big Brother* and mess around in their 'chat rooms'.

I go to the pool for a quick swim and then return to the huge Jacuzzi. It is full of beautiful male bodies and a steady stream of hunks, always naked, climb in and out. No one speaks. Everyone luxuriates silently in the warm bubbling water.

I do confess to noticing and admiring the athletic male body. I can understand why Spartan warriors took young male lovers. This is now considered, of course, to be the ultimate act of criminality. If you take a photograph of a naked twelve-year-old boy in a swimming pool it can send Boots' photo lab scurrying along to the Met, who then arrest you, without further investigation, for sex abuse. A policeman then earns £50 from the *Daily Mail* for passing your name to the newspapers.

In my younger days, the only reason why we were not obsessed with homosexual politics is that no one had invented words like 'homophobe'. In the mainstream we knew that it went on – but we just avoided it. We could look after ourselves. Morbid fascination with finding abuse round every corner did not exist. It was just prohibited and that was that. Unfortunate experiences happened, but no one thought it would ruin the rest of a man's life, nor did men wake up and suddenly find the courage after a lapse of thirty years to go running off to the police.

As I understand it, we are not allowed to call people homosexuals these days. It is not politically correct. They now have to be called people with 'an orientation towards people of the same sex', or 'OTPOTSS'. The anagram for otpotss is of course tosspot. I read that the Metropolitan Police have set up a 'diversity task force' under Commander Cressida Dick to root out 'homophobes'. The Metropolitan Police do very little about burglary or mugging but they have a diversity task force working against homophobia; it is a new 'hate crime'.

As I was putting this journal together, I came across the government's published 'Explanatory Notes' which accompany the Sexual Offences Bill – a landmark piece of

New Labour legislation in favour of OTPOTSS. This is the measure which legalises sex in public lavatories but makes it an offence – punishable with six months in gaol – for a person, or persons, to make love in their own garden. Clauses 3 and 7 are explained as follows.

CLAUSE 3
... where B does not consent to the penetration; and where A does not believe that B consents (<u>subsection (2)</u> – what is said in the note to clause 1 about <u>subsection (2)</u> also applies here), or if a reasonable person would, in all the circumstances, doubt whether B consents and A does not act in a way that a reasonable person would consider sufficient to resolve that doubt (<u>subsection (3)</u>).

CLAUSE 7
... It is an offence for a person (A) intentionally to cause another person (B) to engage in sexual activity (as defined in clause 80) without that person's consent, if he either does not believe that B consents (<u>subsection (2)</u> – what is said in the note to clause 1 about <u>subsection (2)</u> also applies here) or if a reasonable person would in all the circumstances doubt whether B consents and he does not act in a way that a reasonable person would consider sufficient to resolve that doubt (<u>subsection (3)</u>).

It is all very clear; I am sure that young men and women straight out of a club early in the morning will take this

'Explanatory Note' home with them as a guide to their personal behaviour.

It comes about because New Labour does not understand that it is always a mistake, in the English tradition, to codify the common law. A belief in written constitutions is a peculiarly continental aberration but then what can you do with morons who have no sense of history?

This ground-breaking legislation does, however, raise some valid issues, apart from the obvious question as to why it is needed at all.

First, the measure is likely to offend Equal Rights legislation, since public lavatories are presently single-sex institutions – and it will therefore be illegal for heterosexuals to take up their sexual rights. It will be necessary for Gordon Brown, the Chancellor, to finance a nationwide building programme of unisex public conveniences – or Cherie Blair's chambers will bring cases under Human Rights legislation.

Second, unless these unisex public lavatories have provision for wheelchair users, we can expect further legal challenges which would claim that the rights of disabled people to have sex in public lavatories have been infringed.

These changes to our traditional single-sex institutional arrangements will raise many health and safety issues – and the status and pay of lavatory hygiene operatives will have to be improved, causing serious repercussions for public sector pay policy generally.

Finally, I am indebted to Minette Marrin of the *Sunday Times*, who should definitely be appointed to the Number 10 strategy team. She recommends that:

Equal opportunity monitors should visit all lavatories regularly to combat discrimination of any kind. And there will need to be a sex and sanitation auditor called the Cottaging Commissioner tasked with delivering the best possible public lavatory sex experience, given current funding constraints, strongly supported by a new Inspectorate, Oflav.

The Sexual Offences Bill is, of course, a completely demented piece of New Labour legislation, which I suppose will be amended at some stage in its passage through Parliament – or will it?

I wander back down the King's Road after a cup of tea and a lemon cake feeling utterly relaxed. I pass a shop called Zest and go inside to look, rather prematurely I must admit, for an original Christmas present. The shop is crammed with imaginative toys but the one I like the best is the 'inflatable wife'. Underneath the title 'inflatable wife' is written 'totally silent', 'wastes no time', 'spends no money', 'won't crash the car', 'totally faithful' and 'she floats'.

14

A Fishy Story

Iceland was not a success this year. Admittedly our six rods caught sixty salmon, but it was hard work and we were very late each night because our cook in the isolated lodge was Iceland's champion chef. He kept us at the dinner table until midnight eating his delicious dishes and then we were up at seven in the morning. It was exhausting.

Iceland is my favourite country. I love the dramatic countryside, the glaciers and the rivers, the quaint appeal of Reykjavik and the charming people, all 260,000 of them. It has to be my Viking heritage that makes me feel this way. Will I feel the same in Norway?

Returning home, we have to wait nearly two hours to retrieve our bags at Heathrow. I register a complaint with the British Airports Authority, who say it is the fault of British Airways, who say it is the fault of Icelandair's baggage handlers, who say it is the fault of the unions.

In fact, we ourselves are responsible for the chaos and delay on Concourse No. 4 in Terminal 1. We had packed twelve fresh salmon in a polystyrene box, which catches itself in the machinery, jamming the whole system. The other passengers on Icelandair are furious, shouting at the airport staff and swearing that they will never fly into Heathrow again. The only passenger on our flight to remain calm is Björk, the world's number one Icelandic pop star, who exchanges CDs with my son.

Eventually the bags are transferred to Concourse No. 5 and as we retrieve our box the salmon are spilling out all over the floor, which is like a sheet of ice. Everyone is skating around on the contents of our box. Customs are covered in complete confusion. 'You cannot import fresh salmon from Iceland,' they say. 'It could carry the foot and mouth virus.'

I protest: 'Everyone flying in from Iceland comes with salmon in their bags.' They look at me as if I am a raving geriatric. The head Customs man, who is covered in gold ribbons indicating his high rank, goes away to telephone the bureaucracy in head office to see if fresh salmon can be carriers of the foot and mouth virus. Evidently not: our fish, after a great deal of argument, are cleared.

But the policeman at the concourse, who is heavily weighed down with a machine gun, stun grenades, pepper spray, batons, a revolver and handcuffs, says: 'You are utterly irresponsible to put fish in a polystyrene container, they should have been in a wooden box. Next time you come through Heathrow you should behave more sensibly.' He says this with an authority and in a tone which would have done credit to one of Mussolini's Blackshirts. I think silently that he is characteristic of the overpromoted non-commissioned officers that lead our police service. I would mark him out for early promotion to Chief Constable.

15

On the Bus: All Life is There

I set off to lunch at my club on the number 22 bus to Piccadilly, with my Freedom Pass at the ready. On this occasion the conductor seems to have come straight from a party; as we proceed up Knightsbridge towards Hyde Park Corner he entertains us with a virtuoso selection of Irish songs. He never leaves the boarding platform, but clings for dear life to the rail just in front of the luggage rack. I have noticed that a large number of conductors station themselves in this position throughout the journey. Sometimes they deign to stagger a few yards into the lower passenger deck, but never, ever, exert themselves by climbing up to the upper deck to collect the fares. I recommend those who wish to avoid the fare to travel on the top.

At one stage, our conductor gets quite carried away with his tenor voice and it echoes throughout the bus, to much clapping and applause from the many passengers. However, one old lady risks her very life by asking him to lower his voice and return to his arduous duties. The conductor is furious, and in a stentorian bellow tells the old lady to shut up. I am worried that she will be lynched by the appreciative passengers who are not only enjoying a free bus trip, but also have a concert thrown in.

I recall that two days earlier I was on the number 19 with my wife and the bus conductor was an elderly Muslim in a woolly hat with long white bread. I complimented him on his hat and he seemed greatly flattered. It is evidently rare for passengers to engage the conductor in civilised conversation; normally it is an exchange of abuse about the evils of the driver. My wife, for reasons that evade me, is an expert on the Koran and he and she engaged themselves, in front of the other passengers, in a philosophical exchange on the status of women in the Islamic world. The conductor believed that a husband and his wife were the wheels of a bicycle, each dependent on the other; he emphasised, however, that the wife 'had to be the rear wheel, otherwise the bicycle would crash'. The other passengers listened to this insight into Islamic philosophy with bemused looks on their faces, regarding my wife and I with patronising disdain.

Back to the 22 bus to Piccadilly. On this occasion I am sitting on the starboard side. There are hundreds of people shopping in the King's Road; little boys in corduroy knickerbockers play football in the Duke of York's barracks. On the port side sit a thirty-year-old couple, almost certainly unmarried but obviously cohabiting. They seem utterly bored with one another. They are both in informal mufti and presumably have the day off from their investment bank in the City. They do not exchange a word. She is obviously an Oxford graduate and is doing *The Times* crossword. He is reading *Times 2*. We proceed up Sloane Street and at this point the investment banking partnership, very posh, decide to leave the bus – they communicate by some system of osmosis because not one word has passed between them.

With joy I see that the front seat upstairs is free. Sitting across the gangway is a very talkative Middle Eastern gentleman with his attractive bint. It may be the plush décor of the 22 bus which excites him into an endless monologue about money. His lady friend is rather attractive, fifty to fifty-five I would say, unmarried probably, no wedding ring, possibly available for nookie and expensive restaurants when loverboy comes to London. Each sentence spoken loudly on the bus ends in the cost: 'Do you remember that dress in Paris which cost £2000?' 'Let's go to Sotheby's for lunch. We can have a sandwich and a drink for £50.' The lady wears red bootees with elongated spikes which go for a toe. Yes, she is definitely eligible for a warm afternoon in a hotel bed.

My Arab neighbour announces that he is going for two weeks to Mauritius but does not say whether his lady friend is invited or whether that is where he parks his wife. The lady says she is going to the Seychelles to stay with friends for four weeks in their rented villa. 'Your host must be very rich,' says the Arab. 'Yes,' she replies. 'He has four children and he has taken the property for two months.' 'Gracious me,' says the Arab, 'he must be loaded.'

By this time the bus is stationary, having taken ten minutes to travel a hundred yards up Sloane Street. The congestion never varies at this point. It is always caused by a stream of chauffeur-driven Mercedes exiting down Basil Street, with expensive-looking ladies in the back following their week's shopping expedition to the Egyptian bazaar called Harrods.

16

HRT Singles Bars

Those women, sitting bored in the back of their chauffeur-driven Mercedes after their pointless visits to the food hall in Harrods, have given me the germ of a business idea.

It is to build an international chain of singles bars for women in their late middle age; these singles bars would be exclusively available to women on hormone replacement therapy – and they would be known as 'HRT Singles Bars'. There would be no membership fee but entrance would be permitted only on presentation of a doctor's certificate for HRT. The door would be guarded by a retired police person from the Met, and, hopefully, Commander Cressida Dick could be successfully head-hunted from the Metropolitan Police as the first Membership Secretary.

The reason for this exclusive membership requirement lies in the magic qualities of HRT. Crotchety old crones are transformed in a few months into lively, sexually alert female predators seeking out every opportunity for their final fling. How, without this international chain of HRT singles bars, are these women – utterly bored with their husbands, who spend all their waking hours on business –

to find a man? The HRT singles bars will provide the envi-ronment, atmosphere and facilities for easy assignations of an afternoon.

But what about the men? How are they to be recruited? Surely the HRT singles bars must not acquire the reputa-tion of being meeting places for lesbian ladies. HRT lesbian bars might be the Phase II of my business empire.

No – the men will be recruited on the same principle as the women – by the same miracle of modern science.

Only men who can produce a doctor's certificate to Commander Cressida Dick (Metropolitan Police, retired) proving that they are regular takers of Viagra will be admit-ted. Only men with the inexhaustible energy and staying power provided by this drug are worthy of these women doing their time on HRT.

Nowadays more money is made by franchising than by providing every facility directly, so I shall offer Ann Summers, Agent Provocateur, Bradleys and La Perla opportunities to display their wares in glass cases around the walls of the entrance lobby – indeed I might even offer kiosk facilities for the merchandising of appropriate cloth-ing and mechanical toys.

No sex will be permitted on the premises, but substan-tial discounts will be negotiated with a raft of Knightsbridge hotels for short-stay visits in the afternoons. The secret of hotel profitability is, of course, to fill spare capacity in the slack period during mid-afternoon so that I anticipate receiv-ing substantial kickbacks from the Knightsbridge hotel industry. I must check with Commander Cressida Dick, however, that the Crown Prosecution Service will not come on to me for running a call-girl racket for these bored Harrods wives; surely readers will recall the problems encountered by Catherine Deneuve in the film *Belle de Jour*?

I anticipate making a considerable fortune while at the same time offering a real service to the 'Saga generation' who have been completely neglected by New Labour. The HRT singles bars will not be open in the evenings, as a central principle of what I offer – based on the highest moral principles, of course – is to get these women back home, looking flushed and pretty, in time to change for dinner. There they will sit silently, beautifully and attentively while their husbands bore on about the fantastic clever business deals that they have transacted that day for their doting wives. I shall become rich and many failing marriages will be revived.

17

The Titanic Syndrome

It's all very well learning how to dance and play bridge but what happens if the ship hits an iceberg in the Arctic Circle? Can I swim? With the breaststroke I can just about struggle, utterly exhausted, along two lengths of the pool at Holmes Place with my head out of the water like a demented seal; but is that good enough? I have noticed that in every marine accident the lifejackets cannot be found, the machinery of the lifeboats jams, the ship's waiters panic and most of the passengers have to jump overboard and swim, leaving the women and children to fend for themselves. Obviously I need a swimming lesson before this cruise. The *Titanic* here I come. There is a subsidiary reason for some professional coaching. There is something peculiarly horrid about sharing a public swimming pool with other people. I can handle pensioners in the midafternoon who do the breaststroke exceptionally slowly with their heads out of the water, just like me, but come the evening the pool is invaded by athletes from the City. These maniacal males dive in, displacing water like a Krakatoa eruption and then they thrash the otherwise

placid water into a cyclonic Force 10 gale (note navigational terminology).

I get water up my nose and I want to shout out 'you
miserable bugger – stop thrashing the water into a foam',
but I am frightened of these waterborne thugs and
muggers. That is bad enough, but worse still is being
humiliated by gorgeous, sleek, bronzed young female
investment bankers in plastic caps and eye goggles who put
their heads down in the water and do ten lengths before
you can say, 'Hi darling – I'm John.'

Now it so happens that possibly the world's most
famous swimming instructor, Pierre Gruneberg, he of the
Grand Hotel du Cap (Ferrat) is coming to the Savoy to
give lessons, so I enrol. He has taught all the most famous
people in the universe to swim: Picasso, Elton John,
Marilyn Monroe, Charlie Chaplin, David Niven, Aristotle
Onassis, Shirley Bassey, the ex-crown Prince of Albania,
etc. You name them, he has taught them.

So I arrive at the Savoy carrying a little bag belonging
to my grandson and am directed to a designer cubicle on
the top floor. I emerge wearing a Savoy gown to encounter
two very porculant tycoons with bulging midriffs sitting
around and waiting – they have clearly prepared themselves
for the ordeal by eating a heavy meal at the Savoy Grill as
both of them are smoking huge cigars. Tycoons, cigars and
the Savoy Grill go together like pork and apple sauce.

Then Pierre Gruneberg breezes in – all bonhomie.

'Hello, Pierre,' I say as I have met him before at the
Grand Hotel du Cap; the tycoons grunt. 'Good afternoon,' says Pierre. 'I am very pleased that you all want to

I encounter two very porculent tycoons with bulging midriffs awaiting their swimming lesson. Tycoons, cigars and the Savoy Grill go together like pork and apple sauce.

learn *la Méthode Gruneberg*. In the water,' he continues, 'people have a lot of problems because they breathe incorrectly. They have a lot of worries: fright of water, fear of lack of air, claustrophobia, sharks and jellyfish. I don't think there are any sharks in the Savoy pool. Ha ha! So you may survive the afternoon.' The tycoons are not amused – they think that the joke about sharks is at their expense.

Pierre explains that the first lesson is to sing and blow bubbles into a big salad bowl; then you plunge your face into the said bowl and blow bubbles again like a little girl in the bath. The tycoons look as if their dignity is being affronted. Pierre, who has dealt with self-important businessmen like this before, says 'imagine the salad bowl is a champagne glass'. The idea of plunging their ugly faces into a bowl of champagne registers as familiar territory – and the tycoons relax and smile.

It would be tedious to describe the full lesson; suffice to say that within half an hour I am doing the crawl, face down, up and down the pool, breathing in and out like a young female investment banker. Next time, one of them will emerge from the water and say with admiration, 'Hi, John, I'm Jessica from Morgan Stanley.' My heart will beat faster. But more important still I am truly prepared for the cruise, ready to meet any maritime catastrophe. Pierre Gruneberg presents me with this '*Livre d'Or*' entitled *Chanter dans l'eau* and inside he has inscribed, 'To Mr John Nott, *la souvenir de nos premières bulles – très sportivement – Pierre.*'

18

The King-Emperor rules
– over Tooting

Following my experience in Clapham Junction, I was told that if I wanted to see modern Britain I should visit Tooting, so I set out on the Northern Line to reach my destination. On the seven seats opposite me in the Underground, I count two African boys, a Chinese girl, a Europeanised Indian girl in a baseball cap, a veiled Indian lady drinking Five Alive through a straw, and two African girls with hugely extended fingernails.

The first surprise as I leave Tooting Broadway station, standing right in front of me, is a huge statue of Edward VII, Queen Victoria's troublesome son Bertie. Although the Tooting community seems to be three-quarters dark-skinned, mainly Asian, it somehow seems appropriate that the King-Emperor should stand watch over all these relative newcomers from the British Empire.

I wait at the bus stop to take the bus towards Tooting Bec, and get into conversation with a delightful Muslim girl who is covered in black from head to foot, with a black headscarf. She is not a bit fazed at being approached by a white English gentleman, and tells me that, although Tooting is interesting, I will have much more fun if I visit Green Street Market near Upton Park in the East End. So I set off to crisscross London on the Underground.

Before leaving Tooting in south London, however, I visit two markets and note several interesting stalls. The prevailing impression is that much of the population of Tooting spends Thursday mornings in 'nail bars'. I see at least six of these establishments, and they are all full, with long queues; assorted expert Chinese and Indian manicurists, all wearing masks, are busy at work. There is the 'Kim Vi Nail Bar', which specialises in 'acrylic tips and pedicure'. Just opposite this nail bar is the 'Bohas Hair and Beauty Salon', where two Jamaican hairdressers are struggling to plait the very long and wiry hair of their compatriots. The sight reminds me, in the intensity and concentration required, of root-canal treatment at my dentist's. All along this parlour are '100 per cent jazzy soft and silky human hair packages' of every colour of the rainbow, with another specialist packet containing 'new yaki platinum 100 per cent human hair'. Very puzzling. There is a big notice outside this shop stating 'senior citizens on Tuesday, Wednesday and Thursdays – straight or curly perm *ONLY* £22'. I am nearly tempted.

There must be a large Hindu community in Tooting, as one butcher's shop has placed along its counter, in full display and in contradiction to Muslim practice, eight huge great pigs' heads, which stare at me as if they had been guillotined during the Terror of the French Revolution. There are butchers' shops everywhere, and to my surprise they are all staffed by young white men – almost uniquely in the market.

But it is time to set off for the East End. As we approach Upton Park we pass through Whitechapel, Stepney, Bow, Mile End and West Ham – and here the Underground passengers quite suddenly and startlingly become white. The atmosphere changes and it reminds me of *EastEnders*, my wife's favourite television programme. As I get off the train there is a big notice saying that this is the home of West Ham United Football Club.

Green Street is indeed something of an education. It is another Little Asia, a cultural mix of Muslim, Hindu and Sikh but with a solid leavening of Africa. Just as in south London, here in the deepest East End it is the nail bars that are most evident. But here, alongside the nail bars, are many shops and stalls selling wigs (£15.99 to £21.99). I wander in to 'Beauty Queen Cosmetics Number One' to look around. 'Can I help you?' says the elderly Pakistani in charge. 'No, thank you,' I reply. 'I'm just looking around.' He stares at me and says: 'Oh, I thought you wanted a wig.' It is strange, because all the wigs and tresses are obviously made for women. At the exit to the shop are sold expensive-looking magazines aimed at black people, with names like *Black Beauty*, *Black Tress*, *Hyper Hair* and *Black Hair Style and Care Guide*.

The market in Green Street is vibrant and rather noisy – much more so than in Tooting. But it is also wholly African and Asian, selling the usual fare. There are several fish shops, with a lot of smoked fish, fish heads (three for £1), snapper and Indian mackerel.

By this time I am feeling hungry. I am tempted by a shop called Duncan's Pie, Mash and Eels, but decide instead on Kebashi, where I have an excellent curry for £6. As I am eating it, I think how foolish I had been to holiday recently in India. The Oberoi Rasvilas in Jaipur cost me £200 a night and was full of Europeans. Next time I decide to make an authentic visit to the real India I shall travel for free on the London Underground, with my Freedom Pass, to drink in the atmosphere of the Tooting and Green Street markets. As a visitor, you see far more white people in Jaipur or New Delhi than you can ever possibly encounter in Tooting or Upton Park. Somehow I realise why England is such a magnet for immigrants: here it all is, ethnic food, markets, clothes, music, fashion – all similar to the towns of Asia but no obvious signs here of poverty and dereliction.

But even more attractive is the atmosphere – friendly, noisy, vibrant, endlessly fascinating. All these post-war immigrants have brought a real energy to England. You can see it, too, in the Green Street Library in Upton Park, where rows of young Indian and African boys explore the world on the library's computers, supervised on this occasion, as I see very well, by a young twelve-year-old Muslim girl, clad from head to foot in black, who hurries between one station and another, giving advice and help.

So, with reluctance I abandon these markets in south and east London, thinking to myself how excellent it is, after all those drab supermarket visits, to be back in proper markets once again, similar to those you still find in France and Italy – markets that have been destroyed in England by our dreadful supermarket culture.

19

The Majesty of the Law

On the spur of the moment I decide to attend a meeting about Iraq at the International Institute for Strategic Studies. Mr Blair, on President Bush's instructions, wants to invade Iraq, but I am opposed to military intervention, as I believe it could destabilise the whole Middle East; and how can intervention by the Americans do anything other than escalate Islamic extremism all around the world? The replacement of the doctrine of deterrence with pre-emption – the doctrine of pre-emptive war – will bring about an unstable and dangerous world. It is the same tactic that the Japanese used at Pearl Harbor, and it failed. Deterrence proved its efficacy in the Cold War.

We have unfinished business in Bosnia, Kosovo, Afghanistan and Palestine, and now the Americans imagine that they can introduce a liberal democracy in Iraq and police the Middle East – it beggars belief. Have they never studied the British mandate in Palestine and 150 years of our attempts to stabilise Afghanistan? So I attend this meeting to hear a senior member of the US administration, Paul Wolfowitz, explain how the Americans see themselves bringing about 'a strategic transformation of the whole region'. What nonsense he talks.

There is the usual crowd here – socialite millionaires, ambitious businessmen, retired Foreign Office mandarins, politicians of the Hurd and Mandelson variety and a huge posse of television commentators, cameras and equipment. It is a complete waste of time, all laid on for the press. I escape as soon as I can do so. I am out of this world and feel nothing for it. Is it shyness or arrogance? I am not sure which. What I do know is that if I was Defence Secretary I would resign rather than send British soldiers to war without verifiable legal justification and the full-hearted consent of the British people. Mr Blair's evangelism – his post-imperial do-goodery – must be resisted.

I realise that the meeting is near the Temple, so I decide to lunch at the Inns of Court. I became a barrister when I left Cambridge and I paid my dues as a Life Member of the Inner Temple. It seems ironic, in view of my recent visits to our ethnic markets, that I was advised in 1958 by a senior judge to join the Inner Temple rather than Lincoln's Inn, because 'we try to keep the black men out'. It could be described as a policy failure!

Last time I lunched there was thirty years ago and it was grim. The lawyers around me talked unceasingly about their legal cases; they just bored on and on. So my visit today arises out of curiosity and convenience, not pleasure. However, the lunch is excellent: the food is good and the company congenial. Four (young) barristers in their fifties, all quite senior members of their profession, never talk about their cases. I can see that they are good lawyers, and for the right fee could prove that Abel was the murderer of Cain. We exchange gossip about the judges we have known and their peculiar idiosyncrasies.

I say that it is all very disturbing when I find that many of my Cambridge contemporaries are now Lords of Appeal – I shared supervisions at Trinity with a rather ordinary young man who has now become a Law Lord – and I am just the author of a pensioner's chronicle. The Bar is a very closed, incestuous world – and that is from where we draw our judges. In this sense the Bar bears some resemblance to Westminster, but Westminster consists of 'all manner and sorts of men' elected by the people, whereas the Bar, while not entirely a public school enclave, behaves like one. I think we must make a move towards electing our judges – shock, horror! Some of the present ones are out of touch and out of control.

The present Lord Chancellor and Lord Chief Justice, in their isolated, liberal world, have much to answer for. Lenient sentencing may have its merits when overcrowded prison life seems a sure way of encouraging reoffending, but common sense tells most of us that it is foolish to publicly *talk* about lenient sentencing if you are a judge responsible for administering the law. But then, I suppose that a First at Oxford and a life at the Bar are inimical to what passes, outsides the Bar, for common sense. If the European Convention on Human Rights requires a wholly independent judiciary, who will control the judges? *Quis custodiet ipsos custodes?* – Who will guard the guardians? We cannot always be sure that the Home Secretary of the day, a creature of the democratic process, will always be as admirable and determined as Mr Blunkett.

I see, however, that the Home Secretary shares my scepticism about the Judiciary and that he is about to advertise a 'Judge Offer' in the *Guardian*. I recommend as follows: 'Hey, you. Wanna be a High Court judge? Are you twentysomething, black, a single mother and your lover's in Dartmoor for selling coke? You're just the kind of judge we want in tomorrow's modernised legal system. Come and see us. Room 2610b at the Home Office.'

20

Bible Class in Chelsea

I set off to a Bible class at the chaplaincy of the Royal Hospital, Chelsea; I choose it rather than the Alpha Course at the Holy Trinity, Brompton. I have been before and found it really stimulating, principally because the ladies present, ranging in age from fifty to eighty-five, are highly intelligent. Several times I receive insights into the corners of the human experience and the human mind that I could hardly get anywhere else. You don't get these insights from men.

On this occasion we have a discussion about the Books of Ezra and Nehemiah in the Old Testament, which roughly cover the years from 538 to 433 BC. Ezra follows the Book of Chronicles, which closes with Nebuchadnezzar's destruction of Jerusalem in 587 BC and exile in Babylon. Then Ezra and Nehemiah describe the three-stage return of the Jews to Israel and the rebuilding of the walls of Jerusalem. What I find so interesting is that when Cyrus, King of Persia, overthrew the Babylonian empire in 539 BC, he not only allowed the exiled peoples to return home but also encouraged them to practise their own religion.

What we see in Ezra and Nehemiah is an Israel cut down to its roots (only fifty thousand returned from exile) but drawing new vitality from the Mosaic law and growing in the Judaism which for better or worse forms the basis of the New Testament.

Of course the meeting is also about prayer. 'Was God man-made?' asks an old lady. 'He is only one part of the Trinity,' replies the chaplain, 'and I find that young people, when I instruct them for confirmation, grasp the story of Jesus and the idea of the Holy Spirit but they stumble on the concept of God.' 'Does it matter?' I ask, and wish I hadn't. 'If one believes the story of Jesus and can grasp the resurrection of the Spirit, surely God is not important. Isn't God simply an "idea"? God is love.' To my astonishment, the chaplain nods rather than contradicts. 'We do get so hung up on words.' I want to quote Clem Attlee who, when asked if he was a Christian, replied: 'Accept the Christian ethic – can't stand the mumbojumbo' – but I don't.

Then we discuss the need for silence in the modern world. How do people with families and jobs make the time to just sit back and listen? Most of us, if we pray at all, start with supplication.

VESPERS *by A. A. Milne*

> *Little Boy kneels at the foot of the bed,*
> *Droops on the little hands little gold head.*
> *Hush! Hush! Whisper who dares!*
> *Christopher Robin is saying his prayers.*

God bless Mummy. I know that's right.
Wasn't it fun in the bath to-night?
The cold's so cold, and the hot's so hot.
Oh! *God bless Daddy* – I quite forgot.

Oh? *Thank you, God for a lovely day.*
And what was the other I had to say?
I said 'Bless Daddy', so what can it be?
Oh! Now I remember it, *God bless me.*

Perhaps Christopher Robin should be told that it is best to start with adoration, confession and thanksgiving and only then go on to supplication! It is, after all, the order of the Lord's Prayer.

I say that I find it easiest to communicate with the presence of some external being, not by silence, but by watching a little child or marvelling at a spring morning in the countryside. 'Am I glimpsing God on such occasions?' I ask. 'Oh yes,' says everyone. 'What better way can we find of communicating with God than in absorbing silently, on one's own, the wonders of nature.'

Finally, when we break up, I cannot refrain from telling everyone the excitement that I felt last Sunday when I discovered the 131st Psalm. It seemed particularly to apply to me and I did not see any necessary conflict between a visit to Spearmint Rhino and the lesson on humility that comes from this Psalm:

PSALM 131
Lord I am not high-minded: I have no proud looks.
I do not exercise myself in great matters: which are
*   too high for me.*
But I refrain my soul and keep it low like as a child
*   that is weaned from his*
Mother: yea, my soul is even as a weaned child.
Oh Israel, trust in the Lord from this time forth for
*   evermore.*

Next time we meet I would like to ask what the ladies in the prayer group think about the iniquities of fashion and brands, the pressure to be thin and youthful-looking, the cult of celebrity. We agree that the new Archbishop of Canterbury is an interesting man; we like the idea of a brilliant theologian as the Head of the Church; we don't on the whole like scruffy-looking lefties with beards but, if he smartened himself up a bit, we think he could be just what the poor old Church of England needs.

It was an enjoyable occasion, but I do not think that it advanced very much my enquiries into the spiritual side of life in modern Britain.

21

'Famous for being famous': The Cult of Celebrity

Once upon a time, a journalist, John O'Sullivan, then of the *Daily Telegraph*, said of me: 'There are people in gossip columns who are famous for being famous. But John Nott, Shadow Minister of Trade in Mrs Thatcher's team, is at some risk of being famous for being obscure.' Obscurity suits me, as I do not have much in the way of handsome features, gushing charm or scintillating wit. What I do have, obscurity apart, is a well-developed sense of curiosity, so I decide, as part of my voyage of discovery about modern Britain, to try to grasp what this celebrity business is all about.

What is a celebrity? Who are these celebrities anyway? It is indefinable. You know who they are, and what they are, when you read about them in the newspapers. It has nothing to do with achievement. Classic celebrities are David Furnish, the boyfriend of Elton John, Tara Palmer-Tomkinson, the daughter of a stockbroker, and Christine Hamilton, the wife of a former MP. These people are not failures, they are simply non-achievers. True failure gives real pleasure to the British people. Classic failures are Eddie the Eagle, the Olympic ski-jumping loser, Richard Branson, the failed balloonist, and Gareth Southgate, the World Cup penalty misser. People hold achievers who fail in great affection, more so than celebrities.

I consider whether all this celebrity stuff is simply invented by the media – like politics, it is easy to report by lazy journalists – or whether it is a true part of modern culture. Given the huge sales of *Hello!* and *OK!* I conclude that it must be a genuine phenomenon. Where, then, can I indulge my curiosity about celebrity? Where else but around the clubs of night-time London, and on the beaches where the poseurs go to see and be seen by other famous people. I think of St Barts, maybe Sandy Lane, Barbados, St Geran and Mauritius, but plump for Pamplone Beach, St Tropez, due to its proximity.

Now it so happens that I am the owner of a boat which I keep on the Med near Nice, so a visit to St Tropez – one hour away – is easy. *Forget-me-Not III* is a modest vessel, about 45 foot in length with three berths. She is a huge waste of money, because we only put to sea two or three times a year – but I love her dearly. My rich friends, who know better, say, 'If it floats, flies or f—s, rent it,' but I say that ownership gives me greater pleasure. Much to my wife's irritation, I say that I would like to be cremated in my boat. I would like to be taken out to sea like a Viking warrior, while *Forget-me-Not III* is set on fire with my possessions and concubines around me. I'm sure that this kind of Viking suttee would be considered politically incorrect in the twenty-first century.

When I visit Pamplone Beach by boat to have lunch at Club 55 or the Voile Rouge, I am sadly conscious of the fact, that, at the age of seventy, I have lost interest in women's breasts. On the Mediterranean there is not much else to see. My wife tells me that the Cardinal-Archbishop of Milan, when his meal was put before him, was heard to say: '*Pernice, sempre pernice*' ('Game, always game'). In other words, you can have too much of a good thing. It palls. My curiosity on St Tropez beach is nowadays only aroused by calculating the ratio of the manufactured product to its more natural cousin, the unreconstructed human breast. It is clear to me from annual observations on the Mediterranean that the plastic surgery profession is booming. In the London *Yellow Pages* it is easier to find a plastic surgeon to tamper with a woman's breast than it is to get a plumber to change a washer on a tap.

This year we book ourselves into the Voile Rouge, a celebrity playground patronised by Princess Diana in her freedom days, for a late Sunday lunch. There is a row. My dear wife orders a plate of *spaghetti alla vongole* for 45 euros (£32). She says it is cheap because the *spaghetti à la Farouk* costs 100 euros for two, and anyhow the roses on our table must have cost at least £30 (I am thinking about the cup of tea and KitKat at the Mr Wonderful tea dance in Bromley – cost 70p). We gaze out across the water at two huge yachts – really ocean liners – each with a designer black helicopter on the deck; so cost is relative. I don't think the helicopters have engines; they are there for 'show'.

We are served by a large team of very tall leggy blondes, all young Brigitte Bardot look-alikes, who hand us the menu, the cover of which consists of topless ladies whose bikini bottoms are being removed by the proprietor of the Voile Rouge with a pair of scissors. Was this the reason that the Mairée of St Tropez tried to close him down?

At this point our guest, a surgeon from London, draws our attention to a statue of three well-endowed young angels, above whom is fixed an enormous winged phallus, pointing north. He says that the phallus is 'anatomically incorrect' – and he should know – because the left testicle should be hanging below the right. My education never ceases.

At this point the Voile Rouge tea dance begins. It bears scant resemblance to a Mr Wonderful tea dance in Battersea. At least ten or so bikini-clad young beauties appear from nowhere, from inside various boutiques and off the beach, to dance with any fat, rich punter that they can find. The girls depend on tips and whatever else is offered them, particularly invitations to 'come aboard'. The punters dance cheek-to-cheek with their wives and leer over their wives' shoulders at the girls – so everyone is happy.

I can see that the night-time entertainment is moving in the right direction. It follows a predictable pattern: by the evening everyone is completely trashed, the girls dance on the tables, Taittinger champagne is splashed about like water and money is thrown about by the rich punters as if it were going out of fashion. But the wind is getting up and I have to get *Forget-me-Not III* back in bed before dark, so I pay our bill, £220 for spaghetti for five and one bottle of cheap rosé; roll on 'char and wads' in the civic centre in Bromley.

The men, four of us, make one journey up the beach

to Club 55 – and pass a long procession of celebrities as they preen themselves on the beach. We avert our eyes from the beach at Liberty where assorted poseurs lie around completely starkers. We cannot distinguish one celebrity from another as, without his clothes on, Elton John looks like Tara Palmer-Tomkinson. There are roaming paparazzi with their cameras everywhere, trying to snap an indiscretion. It does seem tough that Fergie was banished from the royal presence when they published pictures of her having her toes sucked by an investment banker. Pretty innocent stuff, I think. But it is probably unwise for minor royals to fraternise on celebrity territory when the paparazzi are hiding around every corner. If you sup with celebrities you need a long spoon. Prince Andrew, you are warned.

22

Night-time London

I t is my good fortune to know a youngish man called
Jamie who has written the definitive guide – the Metro
CrushGuide – to the bars and celebrity clubs of night-time
London. He and his West Country friend, Hugo, offer to
take me from place to place one summer evening. We are
booked into three or more fashion rendezvous.

The only club that I had known was Annabels, and that
was many years ago when I used to drop in with other
nutters after late-night votes in the House of Commons.
To quote Jamie's guide, it is nowadays patronised by 'pent-
house hookers, cholesterol-rich Arabs (the overweight
from Kuwait) and European royalty'. It remains a late-
night haunt for our minor royals and run-down members
of the aristocracy. In other words, it has gone downmarket.

We resolve to start our investigation into this creepy-
crawly world with a curry dinner at Benares in Berkeley
Square – and then move on to Sketch, the Met Bar and
Chinawhite, possibly the three most fashionable celebrity
haunts of the moment. Everything moves so fast these
days, however; by the time this book is published, they

may well have joined Annabels in the dustbin of fashion history.

Sketch is new. It is a restaurant/bar opened by Momo, a Moroccan, who is said to have spent £10 million in getting it up to the starting gate. Certainly if the food is anything to go by – the starters cost around £45 a go – he is going to have a struggle to pay down his debt. Jamie awards a star rating to each club, and this one gets five out of five for 'Getting Lucky', 'Eye Candy' and 'Big Spenders'. The most remarkable feature of the décor is the Gentleman's Convenience. You climb some stairs and are confronted by a large number of six-foot plastic eggs. I enter the stand-up section, where a continual shower, ten feet high, cleanses the facilities – but the shower also cleanses me. I dab my bald head dry with an expensive-looking towel.

The restaurant is packed. Some tables are patronised solely by men, serial bachelors (stags stick together before the rut); other tables seem to be reserved for teams of girlfriends on their night out. The prevailing impression is that this is a club for the thirty-year-old London generation, single, lonely and rich. The young women are well-dressed and mostly pretty, culturally alert thanks to a lifetime study of highbrow magazines like *Cosmo* – all 'love and orgasms'. The girls are all looking for their Renaissance Man, but he is hard to find. We stay for an hour or so, and towards midnight the place is still filling up with newcomers, all looking outwardly cheerful but inwardly, I suspect, are quite lost.

The next port of call is the Met Bar. The whole place seems tired, which also goes for its customers. It is very small, this bar, and people sit around on rather faded red banquettes. The Met Bar boasts a lot of celebrity members, media professionals, models, musicians, film executives and fashion victims, but they say there are 'fewer celebs than in its heyday'. Jamie tells me that all these clubs have a similar life: they start with a bang, with beautiful girls, models, fashion icons and film directors, who are then followed by the City boys, who join to chase the pretty girls; the City boys are followed by the Essex girls, who are followed by the plumbers. He says that today's career girls lead a pretty hectic, testing life and they are all looking for 'the security of a rich man'. This means that they are finding older and older men but not, I think, seventy-year-olds like me.

In the early hours we manage to force our way into Chinawhite (the name for a good class of cocaine apparently). But it is difficult. There is a massive queue outside, for this is Wednesday night – the principal night each week. Three huge great black thugs guard the entrance. As we crash the queue at the invitation of the owner, I hear one impertinent young man bellow, 'Look, it's my f—ing grandad!'

Downstairs it is Sodom and Gomorrah; it must be like this in Hades. The crowd is unbelievable; it is impossible to move at all without pushing and shoving through the throng. The dance floor is packed tight with men and women who cannot dance, so they simply move up and down against each others' bodies. Men with men, women with women, women with men, it hardly seems to matter, as the music plays on at a frenzied and deafening pitch. It is impossible to judge the crowd with any meaning, but the congregation seems to be very mixed, a good turnout from young multiracial Britain, diluted with Euro-trash, off-duty call girls, retired Page 3 models, the inevitable City traders and professional footballers. This club, Chinawhite, is said to have a very exclusive membership, and the waiting list is very long. It speaks wonders for the skills of their publicity machine.

I leave Chinawhite at 2 a.m., after heartfelt thanks to Jamie and Hugo for making this experience available. When I get home my dear wife is waiting up for me; she is convinced that someone will have laced my drink with drugs, and I will have been carted off on a stretcher before the lurking paparazzi. 'Well, how was it?' she asks. I can answer her in one word. I reply: 'Ghastly!'

Colonel Harry Flashman VC (flunky) dragoons halted ladies
into a long line for inspection by The Queen.

23

Tea at Buckingham Palace

My wife and I attend a Buckingham Palace Garden Party. It is nice to be asked. My former constituents, many of them deserving of the highest honours for their devoted voluntary work over very many years, have spent a lifetime longing for an invitation.

I dress up in a heavy woollen morning suit bought for £20 as an ex-hire cast-off at Moss Bros thirty years ago. The temperature is over eighty degrees and I anticipate heatstroke during the course of the afternoon. The Palace Garden is absolutely crowded. Hatted ladies are being dragooned into long lines by important-looking flunkies (ex-Guards officers) wielding rolled umbrellas. The retired officers remind me of Colonel Harry Flashman VC, of Balaclava fame. Through this line of route will proceed Her Majesty, as if inspecting a fire brigade rally on Horse Guards Parade – stopping here, smiling there.

Charles Greville, the famous Victorian diarist and Clerk to the Privy Council, described a conversation with the young Queen Victoria as follows:

'Q: Have you been riding today, Mr Greville?

G: No, Madam, I have not.

Q: It was a fine day.

G: Yes Madam, a very fine day.

Q: It was rather cold, though.

G: (like Polonius) It *was* rather cold, Madam.

Q: Your sister Lady Francis Egerton rides I think, does she not?

G: She does ride sometimes, Madam.

(a pause when I took the lead, though adhering to the same topic)

G: Has your Majesty been riding today?

Q: (with animation) Oh yes, a very long ride.

G: Has your Majesty got a nice horse?

Q: Oh, a very nice horse.'

– Gracious smile and inclination of head on part of Queen, profound bow on mine.

Nothing much has changed; Royal conversations were ever thus.

The most conspicuous guests are the purple-breasted Anglican bishops – always an ornithological attraction on these occasions – and they are quickly surrounded by an interesting crowd of 'ecclesiastical twitchers'. I note the presence of one very senior bishop, who reminds me of a recent drama in the Fens. A local vicar, within this bishop's diocese, was prone to marital difficulties and two wives had deserted him. When I met the vicar, who was in a collar and tie, he was with his newly wedded wife, whom the bishop had forbidden him to marry if he was to keep his parson's freehold – and if he wished to avoid the fire and brimstone of the underworld. Under this lordly pressure the vicar stepped down, against the wishes of his parishioners, and there was a major stand-off between the Church spiritual and temporal. It was this former vicar who told me that he met a local farmer at the cashpoint in the town who spoke as follows:

> *'We're all behind you – Reverend.*
> *We're all behind you.*
> *I'll tell you what – Reverend,*
> *If you'd been a bugger*
> *You'd be a Bishop by now.'*

I don't know why a Buckingham Palace Garden Party should remind me of this story, or of the admirable farmer who obviously took a close interest in the affairs of the Church of England. But it is on such occasions that one glimpses the well-directed humour of the modern world; bishops remain, by long tradition, the butt of many disrespectful jokes.

In an earlier world Samuel Pepys recorded in his diary on 4 October 1660: 'To Westminster Abbey … where I saw the Bishops of Winchester, Bangor, Rochester, Bath and Wells, and Salisbury, all in their habits. But Lord at their going out, how people did most of them look upon them as strange creatures, and few with any kind of love or respect.'

At this juncture I decide to detach myself from ecclesiastical affairs and examine the herbaceous borders which, as always, are absolutely splendid. I then make a circular and anonymous detour to avoid being caught up by some minor royal, whereupon I realise that I have lost my wife. I check out several clusters of provincial mayors, magistrates, high sheriffs and lord-lieutenants, but there is no sign of her.

Over beside the tea tent there are two huge queues –

one for the strawberries and cream and the other for the ladies' loo. At these tea parties the temporary erections, lavatories, toilets, latrines, heads – or whatever they are called in royal circles – always have a queue so long and so slow-moving that many good ladies in all their finery never get to see The Queen at all. Queuing for the loo is all part of the Buckingham Palace Garden Party ritual. It really does need sympathetic attention from some flunkey, perhaps the Lord Chamberlain himself, or maybe the Lady of the Bedpan.

This whole jamboree – which is why I note it in my diary – is part of the *un*changing face of Britain. Long may it continue. Almost no one who attends is 'with it'. Most of the guests have no particular affinity with the modern world. It has all the characteristics of a provincial party for provincial people, and one hardly sees the metropolitan élite, commentators, other members of the chattering classes or hacks from the British press. All this suggests that Mr Blair must get to work and 'modernise' the Buckingham Palace Garden Party, replacing it by a hot-dog-and-burger gig in Hyde Park, thereby bringing this corner of Britain's life more into line with New Labour prejudices.

24

Estuary English

I am standing by a bus stop in Sloane Street beside two schoolgirls waiting for the number 19 bus; the girls seem quite mature and sophisticated but I suspect that they are about thirteen or fourteen years old. Both of them are very neatly dressed in blue and wear long dark stockings. They are each clutching a mobile phone in one hand and chatting together.

I can just about understand Estuary English as spoken by the alumni of Eton and other leading public schools, but these girls gabble away in a completely alien tongue. I know that it is English, because when either of them slows down I can catch an English phrase, but generally they speak at such speed as their words slide together that it is almost impossible to believe that they are educated girls speaking the English language.

Mutations are happening very fast among the young. Their language is so strange and alien to the traditional English ear that I wonder whether, in ten years' time when they are recruited to join the BBC, I shall any longer be able to understand the programmes. BBC English as presently understood will have been superseded by some kind of London *Brookside* or Liverpudlian pidgin. The barbarians are waiting at the gate of Broadcasting House.

I ponder why the English language is changing so rapidly. Of course, it has always adapted to changing times and circumstances, and our colonists, the Americans and Indians in particular, have their own intelligible version of our language. I can understand an Indian or an American very much better than an educated English youngster living in our great cultural metropolis.

I am astonished, for instance, at how many young girls greet their friends in clubs and elsewhere with the welcoming epithet: 'Hi, slag' or 'Hi, bird'. The boys use different words, like 'mate'. 'How you, mate?' 'That's cool, mate.' 'Me and my mates went disco last night, dint we?' 'We was going to the pictures last night.' 'I got off of the bus.'

'Isn't it' has become 'innit'. The English vocabulary has shrunk and the young get along with abbreviations, mouthing half the words used by their parents. The young kids at school can't spell because they use abbreviated words for texting. I think the reason is that in an age of mass communication, video, pop music and texting, a new shrunken language has evolved. The educated young are terrified of being labelled as 'posh', while the uneducated majority are equally concerned at being identified as 'yobs'. So, in the great rush to consolidate into our new classless society, language and accents have to meet somewhere in the middle. The next edition of the *Oxford English Dictionary* must of necessity be half its present size and the editor must be under thirty.

25

Spearmint Rhino

My day starts at the College of Arms, where I meet Chester Herald. Before the cruise to Norway, I want to investigate John Nott, a merchant of Viking origin and Mayor of London in 1362, but his arms were granted long before the College was founded. The library of the College is a remarkable museum of English history, containing the pedigrees of thousands of English families from earlier centuries.

When I leave the College of Arms, I see the Millennium Bridge just across the road. I walk to the middle of it and feel it bouncing up and down. I think of going right across the river to Tate Modern, but the exhibitions on display do not interest me so I reverse my steps towards St Paul's. When I enter the cathedral, to my surprise and disappointment I cannot get inside unless I pay an entrance fee of £5. A canon is making a little speech and is persuading us to kneel in prayer, but I am not attracted to kneeling on the lobby floor, nor to paying £5 for the privilege of saying the Lord's Prayer, so I retreat with the £5 still in my pocket.

When I come out of the cathedral, I wonder what to do next. It is midday and much too early to go to my club for lunch. Then an inspiration comes to me; St Paul's to Tottenham Court Road is via the Central Line, and what better moment to reconnoitre that famous lap-dancing club Spearmint Rhino, at 161 Tottenham Court Road?

Having been charged, or rather discharged, from this place of prayer, I reckon that the pleasures of the flesh might not cost much more than the affairs of the spirit. Sure enough, entrance to Spearmint Rhino does cost more (£10) than entrance to St Paul's (£5) but the atmosphere in this gentlemen's club is infinitely more friendly and seems initially at least much less commercial. I plunge down several flights of stairs over a succession of leopard-skin carpets, past walls adorned with pictures of large women with massive breasts. I then enter a cavernous room very reminiscent of an ancient cathedral. Instead of stained-glass windows picturing various saints, however, there is a sort of murky gloom, like a cathedral, but lit only by coloured revolving lights.

It is Tuesday lunchtime and the place is nearly empty except for the girls. There is a smattering of young men having the set lunch (£9.75). I feel no sense of embarrassment at entering this famous emporium of modern culture; I am on an initial reconnaissance, Army-style. I remember the Army maxim: 'Time spent on reconnaissance is seldom wasted', etc., etc.

No sooner have I sat down in the gloom with my eyes adjusting to the darkness – had I known, I would have eaten raw carrots like Second World War pilots before their night forays – when a very pretty girl, half-dressed, comes along and plumps herself down beside me. She announces that her name is Sarah. 'And I am John,' I say. She is wonderfully easy to talk to and does not ask for anything, not even a drink. I discover that she is a qualified midwife and has just completed over five years' training to obtain her qualification. 'The NHS needs you,' I say. No, she replies; she will never work for the NHS, which presumably has trained her at great expense. 'I am saving up to start a children's nursery of my own in Brighton.'

As the conversation is getting more and more interesting, a loudspeaker announces that Sarah is 'on' for her first dance. She begins to squirm up and down a pole and then, entwining her legs about it, she hoists herself towards the ceiling and swivels round and round to the ground, landing in the splits. The splits are a quite astonishing feat of athleticism.

The loudspeaker comes on again to say that Sarah is about to do her second dance. This time she starts disrobing until she is completely starkers except for a G-string. She then proceeds to perform several antics that are presumably intended to mimic an act of sexual intercourse. Sarah is very attractive, but her whole performance, while very professional, is completely and utterly sexless.

While all this is going on and I am working my way through my glass of lager, I realise that another girl has sidled up beside me and, with a smile, she seats herself right next door. I have to say that she is quite something, a really dishy blonde with a very friendly smile. So once again I start to compile in my fertile brain her curriculum vitae.

She left school, or so she says, at seventeen with seven O-levels and three A-levels and then worked for eighteen months in pensions administration at some firm in the City.

Out with some girlfriends one night, she decided late in the evening's fun to visit Stringfellow's, which she said was absolutely wonderful, and the girls were 'so beautiful'. One of her friends said to her: 'Pamela' – for that is her name – 'why don't you apply for such a job? The girls all earn a lot of money.' So, increasingly bored and frustrated working as a clerk in a City office, she lined up for an audition at Spearmint Rhino. 'Did they ask you how many A-levels you'd got?' I ask. She thinks that is very funny. 'No,' she says, 'they did not appear to be interested in my academic qualifications, but as soon as I began to dance and took off all my clothes they engaged me immediately.' I am not surprised. I make a mental note to put her through my own private audition in due course.

Pam says in the evenings and in her spare time (she works four days on and three days off) she is studying 'cognitive therapy'. 'What is that?' I ask. She smiles and points to her brain. I think for one moment she is hinting that she administers to geriatrics like me. 'No,' she says, 'it is really to help girls with bulimia and anorexia.' Pam tells me that she has been working at Spearmint Rhino for only six days and is loving it. 'I love dancing,' she says, 'and I earn a lot of money.' She is obviously keen on money so, being a really boring old fart, I say to her that it is dangerous to be too keen on money in her new profession and she must not get too greedy or things will start going wrong.

She asks me if I would like her to dance. How could I

possibly say no? She is so very beautiful and lively, no man could refuse such an invitation, least of all a seventy-year-old pensioner going through his male menopause. Helen of Troy – no, Pam – takes me by the hand and leads me, walking close, into a VIP room. I never discover why it is called a VIP room.

She then proceeds to dance – or rather squirm – extremely close to me, and her scent as she nearly touches my cheeks is absolutely stunning. By this time a huge great black gorilla-looking man has planted himself in the doorway of the VIP room to ensure, so I am told, that at no point do I touch her body. Pam then starts to disrobe, and, when this mission is accomplished, she stands in front of me completely naked, and once again she begins to dance. She offers me her bottom – and a very nice one, too – and several times, in deference to President Clinton, she bends her face towards my trousers.

I had decided that my behaviour would be immaculate, partly because this is the way that gentlemen behave on such occasions, but also because I am more than conscious of the presence of the gorilla. I do, however, misbehave in one serious respect when she whispers quite erotic comments in my deaf ear (too much shooting, I'm afraid – next time I visit I must wear a hearing aid). I ask whether all the girls 'shave'. 'No,' she whispers in my deaf ear, which is putting on an outstanding performance at this juncture, 'we can shave or not shave. It is entirely up to us, but I shave because it is nicer for people who want to kiss my pussy.' This is the only incident throughout my visit that could be classed as vulgar. 'Ah, what cabinet ministers are missing in their lunch hour,' so I think.

~ *Mr Wonderful takes a Cruise* ~

When this performance is concluded (it took all of five minutes), I pay her the statutory dancing fee of £20 and return to my glass of lager. By this time it is 1330 hours. I am checking my watch like a good young officer through-out and I have to decide whether to depart down the Tottenham Court and Charing Cross Roads to lunch at my club, The Leg of Mutton, with assorted professors, jour-nalists, ex-ambassadors, field marshals and the rest, or whether it makes more sense to have the set lunch at Spearmint Rhino. I decide to stay where I am, but I think that an old man sitting on his own in a lap-dancing club might look rather sad and lonely. I need not have worried because Pam reappears and sits at my table.

I ask her whether she does any modelling. 'What sort of modelling?' she asks, rather shocked I think. 'You have such a beautiful body,' I say, 'you could make a fortune. What about page three of the *Sun*?' She doesn't like that idea at all. 'I wouldn't want three million people looking at my body,' she says. 'If I did it, I would only do so for a very large sum of money.' I am rather puzzled at this, as she is putting her body on almost permanent display in Spearmint Rhino, and in the most suggestive way, but clearly that is different and more modest to appearing topless in the pages of the *Sun*. At 1400 hours precisely I depart, saying goodbye to Pam, who by this time is being friendly to some young men at an adjoining table.

What do I think of it all? In some extraordinary way it is all utterly respectable. There is nothing in the remotest bit sordid about it. In spite of all the exposed naked flesh, it is remarkably lacking in sexual content. Pam has been a joy to meet: young, intelligent – yes, very intelligent – energetic, personable and quite exceptionally beautiful. I do hope she does well in her life but where does she go next? Isn't it all downhill from here? Maybe marriage and the grinding toil of children?

After my excursion to Spearmint Rhino, I remember reading only recently about the politically correct 'Thought Police' and how they see this male experience. One mental health expert had said: 'Men are becoming vulnerable to behavioural disorder as a result of attending gentlemen's clubs. Such attendance,' he went on, 'is an increasingly prominent phenomenon.' There is 'compulsive sex addiction among British men'; such men need 'to obtain emotional reassurance'. At the Tate addiction clinic in Wales there is a twelve-stage recovery programme for men who have become 'addicted'. 'It is sod all to do with artistry, it is depraved and debasing,' says the blurb for the addiction clinic. Ha ha! I think. It is these politically correct 'experts' who need help. To use their own language, sod the lot of them.

26

The Dartford Dinner Dance

After my visit to Spearmint Rhino I decide to cleanse my soul and visit Mr Wonderful in Dartford. Am I crazy? I am catching the train from Charing Cross on Sunday morning to join a Mr Wonderful 'dinner dance', as the lunchtime session is called. I am surprised and impressed by my determination to get this ballroom familiarisation course behind me prior to the cruise. Will I have the courage to take to the floor – perhaps a glass of Asda Red at lunch will fortify my courage – or would I be better served by an overdose of tranquillisers? I had lost my programme of events, so I telephoned Mr Wonderful himself and received a copy by return, together with a charming note: 'We do hope to see you again, John. I will book you a place at the lunch table.'

The morning of the great day I wake up in a high state of tension. I shave with great care, use a liberal amount of mouthwash from a British Airways travel bag and put on a clean Marks & Spencer shirt. There is a moment of hesitation about my tie. Initially I choose a red one from Austin Reed but then reject it. I am sure my dancing partners will all be closet Tories who have lapsed. I decide that a red tie would give the wrong signal, and I therefore choose a bronze neckpiece with yellow spots. I put on a rather characterless grey suit, very worn, made many years ago by Prince Charles's tailor, Huntsman of Savile Row. But I tear out the Huntsman label because I feel that neither Prince Charles nor his tailor would want their jacket to be seen hanging over a chair at a Mr Wonderful Dinner Dance in Dartford. I hesitate about my shoes because women swoon over shoes and it is the first thing that they notice about a man. I have a very snazzy pair of good-looking Bally brogues, but they make my feet ache and so I discard them for a more homely and comfortable artificial leather pair that I bought at a sale at British Home Stores.

Thus equipped, I present myself at the Charing Cross ticket office for a day return to Dartford – only to be told that there is a special concession for the holders of a Freedom Pass, so my journey costs me nothing. Dartford High Street is almost deserted on Sunday morning except for a gang of youths on skateboards. But as I approach the Acacia Hall I notice a steady stream of pensioners walking – no, waddling – towards my destination. We all climb the stairs with difficulty and pay a £10 entrance fee for dancing, a three-course lunch and continuous music personally supervised by Mr Wonderful. What value one gets at these events! I am allocated table no. 6.

By the time I take my seat, the dance floor is already crowded with at least thirty glamorous young couples (average age around seventy). Mr Wonderful is heard to exclaim: 'If you want to dance, don't come to Dartford because of the crush.' There must be 150 pensioners present, although that is unfair because there is also a smattering of youth (late fifties). Evidently the Dartford dinner dances take place at the Acacia Hall once a month, and people come from all over the south of England. My next-door neighbour Pearl, who is seventy-nine, had taken the train at King's Lynn that morning, changed at Charing Cross and planned to return that night – a round trip, I guess, of several hundred miles. Pearl has left her husband in Zimbabwe and hardly ever sees him, because if he abandons their house for a day, the Mugabe mob would take it over.

On my other side at dinner/lunch sits Jane (seventy-four) who is with her young son, Frank (fifty-four). Jane was married for twenty-five years to Albert, but she got rid of him, 'because he sulked'. Her second husband died and her third husband was a 'rotter'. I ask Jane whether she would marry for the fourth time. 'Never,' she says, 'but I would like a steady companion – as long as he could dance.' She does not look at me, although she does ask me to dance. I protest vigorously that I am incompetent. 'No,' she says. 'You must try.' So I am hauled to my feet and dragged protesting to the dance floor. It is a foxtrot. After I had twirled her expertly around the floor, I ask her how I am performing. 'You are doing what is known as a "one-step",' she says. 'It went out in the 1920s; you badly need lessons.' 'Is there anything helpful that you could say?' I reply. 'Yes,' she says. 'You have the timing and the rhythm, and you are thin.' I am immensely flattered and encouraged by such praise from a professional. Where there is life there is hope.

At 3.30 lunch is ready and we collect it table by table. It is delicious. Wine is provided for free, as part of the £10 entrance fee. I am really enjoying myself by this time. The atmosphere is lovely: so many (young) couples having a great time. I know, at last, that a whole slice of my life has been wasted. Here I am, among my own, back in the suburbs. Why had I been diverted by ambition into climbing the greasy poles of business and politics? Now a whole new world lies open to me, courtesy of Mr Wonderful.

27

Home to Cornwall

I am off on First Great Western from Paddington to Penzance to make this summer's visit to our rural retreat. It is, of course, the most beautiful place in all the world. It is a special time of year, principally because all four grandchildren will be with us. It is also the time of harvest.

How can I explain the sheer pleasure and excitement of the harvest? What can be more wonderful than travelling around the fields with the combine, then seeing the newly combined grain slide through the augers into the storage bins? This farm is my life. We have been farming the land here for thirty years and I do not regret a moment of it, but nowadays it is impossible to make a profit. There are 120,000 farmers contributing just £1.7 billion to the national economy; but the food industry is vast, worth £65 billion and employing half a million people. If farmers increasingly decide it's a mug's game and tire of producing food without a profit, there will have to be mass imports of food and the food processing sector will go abroad, probably to France. We have done everything on our farm: beef, early lambing, horticulture. Now we just grow cereals – and

I draw social security benefits from the European Union for doing so.

With wheat at £50 a tonne it is an expensive indulgence; it is cheaper to keep a mistress in a love nest in Earl's Court than grow cereals on a farm in southern England. The difference is that when the wheat is safely gathered in, it is silent; it does not bleat on, wanting to be taken on holiday and otherwise indulged. So the choice between keeping a loss-making farm in Cornwall or an expensive mistress is an easy one. Wheat wins every time.

28

Saffron Gets a Pellet up her Nose

First drama of the family holiday. Emergency. My five-year-old granddaughter skilfully manages to get a small plastic pellet from her cousin's gun up her nose. Panic. Screams. Her grandmother dashes over in a panic too, making everything twice as bad as it needs to be.

'There's a pellet up my nose!' my granddaughter screams. 'Where? Where?' screams her grandmother. Total chaos. 'Blow your nose! *Blow your nose!*' More screams, more panic. Quick high-level conference with my daughter-in-law takes place. She remains relatively calm. She and I decide to go to the local surgery. It is closed. The place is run by a 'receptionist' whose principal function is to make life easy for the doctors who nowadays seldom, if ever, make a home visit to the sick.

So we set off to the casualty department at the local hospital. The NHS, encouraged by the consultants at the hospital factory in Truro, has tried for thirty years or more to close our local hospital, but the community would rather die in its own hospital than be saved in the main health factory forty miles away in Truro.

We arrive at casualty, where we are met by a very helpful assistant who fills out a form. We wait. By this time my granddaughter seems to have recovered from the drama. We wait. And we wait. Although we imagine that we are the front of the queue in casualty, others are ushered in before us. After an hour, we are directed into the hallowed halls of casualty. There are a number of friendly ambulance drivers standing around, and a few people who appear to have broken their limbs. We spy a doctor – he is Indian – who is filling up endless forms, writing letters, looking up files and making telephone calls. It is very like casualty in Kathmandu or Kerala. There is nothing wrong with the atmosphere, which is cheerful and friendly, but one simply feels that one is visiting an Indian bureaucracy rather than a hospital.

My daughter-in-law makes an interesting observation. She says that to become a doctor in England you need three straight As in your A-levels to get into medical school. When you get out the other side of five years' training, you are well qualified to be a professor or a research doctor in some obscure laboratory. Our nurses now have university degrees; I wonder why?

When eventually our Indian doctor manages to extricate himself from his paperwork, he has a lovely bedside manner. He sets about putting my five-year-old granddaughter at her ease. He is patient, quiet and kind. He has all the peaceful qualities and demeanour of his race. My five-year-old granddaughter is really forthcoming to our Indian doctor, the only one on duty in casualty to cover a community of more than a hundred thousand people; he's infinitely better qualified to deal with patients than an over-educated English medical student. I suspect that he has a real interest in what he's doing, and he will not be tempted to become a consultant in private practice, where he can rip off the private insurance industry. The thought of all these expensive private consultants in Harley Street reminds me of Hilaire Belloc: 'They murmured as they took their fees … there is no cure for this disease.'

The casualty doctor looks in my granddaughter's nose. Nothing can be detected. He suggests we go to ENT in Truro. We take the decision *not* to take her to the ENT consultant in the hospital factory forty miles away. 'It is your risk,' he says. We understand. The thought of an ENT consultant stuffing the latest piece of technology up my granddaughter's nose is more than we can bear. As we leave the local hospital we wonder, why could not a nurse look up the child's nose? Perhaps she has not got a degree in nasal science. Such a simple thing to do; we could do it ourselves had we possessed the right equipment.

So this is a microcosm of the NHS: lovely people, friendly nurses, a pleasant Indian doctor. But it is clear that after every patient he sees he has to fill out a mass of forms in triplicate, in case we sue the poor man for giving us the wrong advice. My doctor friends tell me that the NHS is being crippled by litigation – a nasty disease which we have imported from America. No one benefits except the lawyers. What a mess, what a mess.

29

Countryside Stewardship

I have devoted forty years of my life to improving conservation and wildlife on my farm. I have taken out a few poor hedges to create larger economic fields (before the regulations would have stopped me doing so) but I have established large areas of hardwoods, planting at least ten thousand trees. The trees provide a haven for wildlife, particularly for rabbits, which graze on the field margins all around the farm. I learned that the government, poor fools, would pay a subsidy to farmers on the basis that the field margins (6 metres) are left free of crops. If governments want to subsidise rabbits, I thought, it was OK by me.

So I set out to join a European Union-sponsored scheme called the Countryside Stewardship Scheme. It sounds good, doesn't it? It is the latest fad for government-appointed conservation quangos and New Labour itself. After several inspections by pleasant conservation field officers, and a really helpful visit by a lady from the Farming and Wildlife Advisory Group, I received an 'Offer', which would have subsidised the rabbits – or is it me? – to the tune of £4000 a year, a much-needed boost to the farm finances.

But when I receive the 'Agreement' for signature, I cannot understand how anyone could be so desperate for a subsidy that they would sign away their freedom and property rights by joining such a scheme. Subsequently I have a nice letter from Mrs Beckett, the caravanning Secretary of State, sympathising with my objections but pointing out that thousands of farmers have already signed up to the scheme. Poor fools them; I fear they are desperate for money in the current farming crisis. But for me it is nationalisation of my land by another name. It opens up my farm to inspection and 'monitoring' by unknown bureaucrats; it requires a mountain of additional needless record-keeping; it freezes the farming into a set pattern; and then it caps it all by listing the Acts of Parliament that constitute 'Good Farming Practice' on my farm. These are the Acts in my 'Agreement', which I must read, study and obey – there is not much time left for farming: the Wildlife and Countryside Act 1981; Part III of the Food and Environment Protection Act 1985; the Heather and Grass etc. (Burning) Regulations 1986; the Water Resources Act 1991; the Control of Pollution (Silage, Slurry and Agricultural Fuel Oil) Regulations 1991; the Clean Air Act 1993; the Crops Residues (Burning) Regulations 1993; Ancient Monuments (Class Consents) Order 1994; the Plant Protection Products Regulations 1995; the Hedgerow Regulations 1997; the Groundwater Regulations 1998; and the Action Programme for Nitrate Vulnerable Zones (England and Wales) Regulations 1998.

Then it says that, in addition to abiding by the above Acts, I should also follow the standards of Good Farming Practice and, to avoid prosecution on my own farm, I should 'protect and maintain' any 'traditional' items such as 'walls, woodlands, hedges, hedgerow trees, ponds, wetlands, bogs, marshes, osiers and withies, ditches, dykes, rhymes, limestone pavements, cave entrances, swallow holes, sand dunes or areas of bare ground, mud flats, shingle and ungrazed salt marsh'. I think the draftsmen are completely bonkers. As if I would not do all these things anyhow. I own this property.

Then, buried away in the Schedules, are some real scorchers. On 'lowland pastures', as defined, my cattle must graze for a period of at least ten weeks to achieve 'an average sward height of between 50 to 100 mm'. The cattle must, as well as ensuring that the grass is not grazed of course to a height of 49 mm (that would be grounds for prosecution) also be particularly careful when the ground is wet – the cows must remember this – to avoid 'poaching'. So this Agreement goes on for thirty pages of the most detailed and wholly impractical requirements for farming on my own farm.

It is a conservationist's dream and a practical nightmare, setting out a whole series of utterly futile tasks, subject always to prosecution if they are not attained. It is, of course, devised by lawyers on the instruction of civil servants and English Nature. President Mugabe could not achieve so much with so little bureaucratic effort; he has so much to learn from the British government.

In the last resort, it is the proud ignorance – or is it the proud insolence? – of the town-based bureaucracy that always knows better than people on the ground. Control, control, control, and English Nature will create a beautiful conservationist heaven but a farming wasteland, dominated by weeds. Presumably it is assumed in Whitehall that we will never need our farmers again.

As I write this I hear from the chief executive of our local council that he conducted recently a survey of rural businesses in our area. There are six hundred farmers in the district, and 75 per cent of them are just breaking even, or losing money. The heart of west Cornwall is being torn out.

30

Badgers

As I come down the farm lane, I see a huge pile of earth and stones right in the middle of the road. 'Oh my God,' I think, 'a badger.' Sure enough, a quick examination reveals five or six newly dug entrances to a badger sett. I like the look of a badger as much as the next man. They are an attractive part of the animal kingdom. Unfortunately they are a pest and a confounded nuisance.

Thirty years ago there was unquestioned evidence that badgers were spreading bovine TB to cattle. When I had a beef herd it caused no great problem other than an annual test conducted by the local vet on behalf of the Ministry of Agriculture. On one such occasion, we had our young Hereford bulls in the farmyard undergoing the test. Then the stock bull, a huge great animal, escaped from the cattle crush. A mighty fight arose between father and sons, not something at which you want to stand around and be taken out in a family punch-up. I read a lot these days about domestic violence. The stock bull was furious with his sons and, seeing a spanking new Mercedes in the corner of the yard, he crashed straight into it and sat on it with a frightful crunch. Its German owner, who was renting a holiday cottage, burst into tears. His pride and joy had been destroyed by an English bull – retribution for the Second World War, I thought.

Anyway, back to TB in badgers. At that time, before the supermarkets set about destroying British agriculture (indeed, worse, they have destroyed much of the prosperity and way of life of rural England), I was surrounded by dairy herds built up over generations with much love and pride. The dairy herds were being undermined, if not decimated, by bovine TB in badgers. Then a great uproar arose among the animal lovers in the towns and a Tory government, the genesis of many of our rural woes, brought in special protection for the badger with the Protection of Badgers Act 1992. These same badgers that were threatening the livelihood of farmers in the district were then able to roam freely over the fields, dropping their faeces in the path of grazing dairy cows, smashing down chicken runs and uprooting crops. The lovely little badger is a pest.

Today, some thirty years later, no government has the guts to confront the ignorant urban animal lover and accept the obvious problem – the need to reduce badger numbers – so it forms and re-forms scientific studies to avoid the issue. The latest is the Krebs Committee.

Seeing the new badger sett under construction, I decide to move it on. But I have no great desire to break the law, so I contact the Ministry of Agriculture, now called DEFRA, in Bristol, which is 150 miles from where I live, and eventually a massive form arrives. This form I duly complete and despatch. No word from Bristol.

The badger continues to obstruct my farm lane, which is used not only by me but by ramblers. I can be put in prison if I obstruct a rambler. In due course, after at least three weeks having passed and when I am away elsewhere, arrangements are made by Bristol for a conservation officer to inspect the badger sett. A lady who, no doubt, is weighed down by academic qualifications, comes and makes her judgement. She will report.

Further weeks pass, and then a licence to 'interfere' with the badger sett arrives. It is signed by the 'Wildlife Administration Unit'. How can an administration unit in Bristol operated by civil servants 'regulate' wildlife? It is completely daft. Attached to the licence is a hugely detailed set of instructions as to how we are to block some badger holes and build a one-way, self-operating door on another hold so that the badger can get out of its home and not get back in. Attached is another form in which we are required to report, in detail, how we have dealt with this badger invasion, so as to show, presumably, that we have treated this cuddly little animal with the courtesy and kindliness which the Wildlife Administration Unit in Bristol requires.

The badger, which is much more intelligent than the civil servants in the Wildlife Administration Unit in Bristol, 150 miles away, thinks that all this bureaucratic regulation is a complete joke. It does not use the one-way, self-operating door because its animal instincts tell it that only humans slam the front door and leave the keys inside the house. Badgers are not stupid. When it wants to leave home, it simply digs a fresh hole so that its return is simple.

My farm manager and I reckon that the cost of all these

forms, visits by advisers, train fares from Bristol, first-class stamps and the time spent in salary hours expended cannot be less than £5000. A further month passes and the badger is perfectly content with its feet up in its badger sett watching the television, or whatever it is that badgers do in their spare time.

In desperation my farm manager telephones a local gamekeeper to seek his advice. 'No problem,' says the gamekeeper: 'soak two potatoes in diesel fuel and put them down the hole; the badger will have buggered off by the next morning.' Can it be true? I let the reader guess.

The badger is perfectly content with its feet up watching
the television, or whatever else badgers do in their spare time.

31

Tea Bags for Two

'Why are you using that tea bag a second time?' asks my daughter. She thinks it hilarious; I think it is a strange question. After all, it is a simple issue of economy. If a tea bag will do two cups of tea it is sensible to save it up for the second cup. My daughter should realise that the manufacturers of Typhoo put more tea than is necessary into a single bag, and I should know; I was once the chairman of that company.

Tea bags are also useful for placing, still warm, on early-morning eyes as a cheap alternative to Optrex. I ponder my daughter's attitude. She is not a spendthrift, she owns her own house in London and has a much larger disposable income than my wife and I ever had at a similar point in our marriage. Perhaps this is why she cannot understand simple issues of day-to-day economy. For instance, turning off the lights, using the minimum depth of bath water (very important, this one), peeling potatoes rather than buying them ready-prepared in a packet, growing herbs and tomatoes from seed rather than buying seedlings in a nursery or, worst of all, in a supermarket.

My children's generation does not understand that today's necessities for them – disposable nappies are a good example – were yesterday's luxuries. I remember when my wife washed the children's nappies by hand, and the thrill which we all felt in the household at the arrival of our first automatic washing machine. Skimping and saving for my wartime generation was the very stuff of life. How can we, after spending a lifetime teetering on the edge of bankruptcy, with school fees, mortgages, farming disasters and leaking roofs, cast off the habits of a lifetime? All war babies still use tea bags a second time, but how can we expect the modern generation to understand?

32

Dad: 'Same world, different planet'

My daughter's attitude to the tea bag makes me ponder further these generational differences. One of the great pleasures of old age is that you have the time to be an observer of the world – to watch young children playing with one another. My two young granddaughters – five and one – really lose themselves in their own private world. My nine-year-old grandson is utterly taken with gangsta rap and its crude, profane and violent lyrics; he comes alive when he discusses hip-hop with his pre-teen cousins. It provokes the same concern among his parents as the Rolling Stones did with mine. All the time, the world moves on.

This passion to emphasise the generation gap is particularly strong among the self-proclaimed 'modernisers' of our day. It has spawned new words, like 'ageism', among the politically correct. My decision to write a journal, to set out on a journey of enquiry, provokes the anticipated and patronising response that it would enable a blinkered old man to go out and see what the 'real world' is really like.

It is essential to the self-esteem of the young that they see themselves as uniquely plugged in to change. It is given added poignancy with the older generation's plodding approach to new technology, the internet, mobile texting and the rest. As my niece said to me the other day: 'The moment that you and the older generation have something in common – you know that you are growing old yourself.'

This struggle for eternal youth – the unending fight against nature – seems to start with the thirty- to forty-year-old generation – the ageing young. They are in a constant sweat that they may be missing something – or someone – better. Flashy adverts encourage them to believe that there is such a thing as perfection in a man, in food, in furnishing, in cars. Never settled, always shopping for designer brands to make them more sexy, more important, forever young – one eye on the main chance. The grass may be greener on the other side, or so they think, until they take up with the next partner who turns out to be just as boringly normal – or as boringly human as the rest. Perhaps it is an argument for a Chinese-style gerontocracy to take control of England, enabling us to put all those patronising and restless youngsters in their place.

33

E-mail

I decide to take a quick look at my e-mail. I have not started the computer for the last two weeks. Counting up the unsolicited junk mail which has arrived for me, I guess there are somewhere in the region of two hundred items. There is not a single personal message at all.

I make a count of the majority issues that comprise my junk e-mail messages. The vast majority are offering me loans at favourable rates of interest: The one thing I do not want at my stage of life is a loan. But there is a fairly large scattering of advertisements for penis enlargement (they must have known). I wish e-mail had been invented when I was in my twenties; had it been, I might well have succumbed to the attractions of this marketing, but at the age of seventy I think penis enlargement has come a little late. I console myself by remembering one of our more sophisticated au pairs who said: 'It doesn't matter if it's small so long as it is cheerful.'

'What's your e-mail?' They all ask this question. I tell them, 'I don't do e-mail.' I only 'do' the telephone, fax and letter. They look at me as if I am really sick and failing.

Nice Indian ladies living in New Delhi, fishing guides in New Zealand, even St Peter awaiting my arrival across the River Styx, all ask me my e-mail address. I have one; but I keep it secret until I am forced to disclose it when booking a cheap seat on easyJet. I realise that this Microsoft intrusion into the former, ordered progress of our lives has taken over everything. But it has not improved our love lives or our sanity one tiny jot. It spawns billions of unnecessary e-mail messages which do nothing to advance the progress of the human race. I am not destructive by nature – although there is a bit of anarchy there somewhere. I will die a contented and happy man if I can do something really useful to help mankind. I am therefore bankrolling a spotty but brilliant and socially dysfunctional sixteen-year-old Chinese student in Taiwan – the Einstein of the future – to produce a deadly computer virus which will lay waste to the internet for ever.

34

My Feral Grandsons

I take my two grandsons on a picnic and barbecue to our Cornish river. It is a lovely spot, about one mile inside a wood. We see a red deer, several pheasants and a few duck. The boys dangle their rods in the river but it is July and the sea trout, all that is in the river at this time of year, are too wild and scared to show themselves by day.

We decide to stay the night on the bunks in the fishing hut. It is primitive but boys between the age of five and ten are completely feral; they do not wash, their hair is normally matted and, if permitted, they quickly revert to the state of cave children. It is important at this period in their lives when their behaviour is indistinguishable from their Stone Age ancestors to introduce them to some of the more unpleasant practices of primitive man – skinning a rabbit, plucking a pheasant, gutting a fish, gralloching a deer.

It is only a question of time, perhaps a few generations hence, before the world reverts to a natural state – chaos – and survival is only granted to those who know how to live a subsistence existence off the land – a totally unimaginable situation to the urban population of today. My wife, who spent her war years on a tiny hill farm in Nazi-occupied Slovenia, has a wealth of knowledge on how to survive – ultimately the only skill that matters. Fifty thousand years of inherited experience and knowledge, passed down through the generations, is now forgotten in favour of the inventions of the modern age; they will certainly let us down.

At four o'clock in the morning, the world outside the hut goes quite mad. Every animal is fighting every other animal. It is the rut and sexually aroused roebuck are causing havoc in the woods, demonstrating their aggressive macho qualities to the expectant and equally randy females at the scene. I observe that when their women are on heat the males of the animal kingdom lose every kind of inhibition and all sense of personal safety and survival. A cock pheasant, in his April mating madness, will attack a gun dog and even a human being, and a buck in mid-July will stand its ground, stamp its feet and stare at a human hunter with patronising contempt. Women are all that matters; life is of secondary importance to the mating imperative.

There is endless, puzzled debate, particularly among sophisticated feminists, as to why men should risk everything – their careers, their marriages, their savings and their solvency – for the sake of 'an adventure'. I fear that it too is a primitive imperative and unless you study the animal kingdom it is not possible to understand the more foolish adventures of the human male – he is as blind to danger as a roebuck in the rut.

The next morning I call in to see the farmer who looks after our shoot in the valley. He is in the middle of a Ministry TB test. A cow starts calving and we have to get the calving machine out. It is a fearsome instrument which we have used many times ourselves. You simply rest it against the backside of the cow and winch the poor calf out into the world. Interesting for the boys, whose knowledge of the world of nature until now has been dominated by sanitised wildlife films on television, museums of natural history and lectures by teachers who have never experienced the rawness and cruelty of nature.

35

White Van Man

On my way back to London from Cornwall I stop off at the Arundel Arms in Lifton for a meeting of the South West Rivers Association. I am driven up there by my farm manager in my very own white van.

I am in love with my white van. I am known in Cornwall as the White Van Man, and my richer acquaintances do not understand why I drive everywhere in this white van rather than in the Mercedes. They do not understand love. You do not ask why someone loves a beautiful woman. It cannot be explained. It is almost inevitable, if she is a beautiful woman, that she spells trouble. I cannot explain my love for my white van; but I do know that my white van will neither let me down nor make impossible demands upon me.

My white van will not ask me to go shopping at Harvey Nichols and expect me to stand around while it tries on a succession of highly expensive dresses, which sell at thousands of pounds because they have a stupid label attached to them. I know that my white van, which is a diesel and is therefore cheap to run, will pass its MoT but how can I be sure that a beautiful woman will pass her MoT unless I get her into my bed, and there is not much hope of that. My white van has all the attributes that most beautiful women lack. The white van is comfortable and silent; it is obedient and stops when you apply the brakes. It belches out diesel fumes, admittedly, but that is better than breathing out champagne fumes. Champagne always makes me feel sick. Yes, I am definitely in love with my white van.

However, I note the following in *The Times*: 'White Van Man is commonly regarded as suffering from every social disability. White Van Man is evolving (Darwin) into Silver Van Man; Silver Van Man has both civility and aspirations.'

Accordingly, my white van has now been sent to a clinic for a complete makeover: colour change, face-lift, breast enhancement, botox injections, bikini waxing with a 'Brazilian', and a protective self-tan. In the back of the van, on the recommendation of my friend Carole Caplin, I am installing yoga mats, meditation kits and incense candles, all intended to produce 'inner calm' and release 'blocked energy'.

My silver van will be 'mutton dressed as lamb' – body beautiful, eternal youth; no one will ever know that it has two hundred thousand miles on the clock with many breakdowns (divorces) in its history on the road.

36

Aliens Arrive from the Country

The King's Road is always busy on a Saturday afternoon; it is a truly wonderful melting pot of urban Britain. It is rare to hear English spoken or what passes as English on the BBC – pidgin English yes, Estuary English sometimes, French, Spanish, Serbo-Croatian, the different languages from the Indian subcontinent – all of these, but English seldom. Islington may be the throbbing heart of political London but the King's Road is the sartorial and linguistic capital of multicultural Britain.

This is the day before the great Countryside March, and the King's Road is invaded by aliens from the English counties, the disenfranchised minority from farms and country villages, and it has taken an overwhelming sense of frustration to get them here. Some of them try to hide their racial (English) origin by wearing gaudy sweatshirts but the majority of the men are in tweed jackets, and the tweed jacket is an alien costume in the King's Road. It is what the burka is to Pamplone Beach or the bikini to Kandahar.

Many of the more elderly persons on that Saturday morning have hairy purple faces and a moustache. It is hard to tell whether these aliens are male or female. My companion remarks that women do not do well in the countryside; they have none of the incentives available in the cities to keep them active, young, slim and pretty. There are no gyms, singles bars, gentlemen's clubs of varying quality and activity, and no lap dancing. None of that in Nether Wallop. On this Saturday morning there is a fair smattering of posh totty, who look much more healthy than their urban counterparts; they appear to be straight off their hunting stallions – or their stallions are just off them – and are raring to go. But generally past the age of thirty it is possible to detect among these rural girls a sense of accelerating decline. Too much spare time, too much gardening and too much drink.

How these country people, part of a minority sect called the English, stick out so much as real foreigners it is hard to say but certainly they seem more alien in the King's Road than any of Mr Blunkett's recent immigrants. A number of country squires can be spotted in bookshops and pubs. Some of them have had too much to drink at lunch. Some have put on very old serge jackets over rather faded and stained corduroy trousers. This mixed garb is an attempted concession to 'town', or a failed attempt to disguise their foreign (i.e. English) origin. The way they walk, dress and speak marks them out as embarrassed immigrants to the great capital city of what was once their country. It is no more.

I think to myself that it would not be beyond New Labour to have published a regulation, something like an EU regulation, which imposes immigration barriers into the main entry points to London to ensure that these strange alien people from the countryside are able to speak the language, acknowledge their sovereign (Mr Blair) and are not carrying infectious diseases (venereal or otherwise) into the capital city.

It occurs to me as I write, in jest, about the arrival of these English countrymen – sorry, countrypersons – into what was once their capital city that any similar joke about our immigrant arrivals would be totally offside – and a humorist would be subject to arraignment before a Star Chamber called the Race Relations Board. I have no hang-up about immigration as, culturally and economically, the overwhelming majority of our arrivals will greatly benefit the country. At least we may avoid the perils of falling population like France and Germany. But it is not a level playing field. For the politically correct, 'multiculturalism' involves applauding all cultures and traditions other than that of the English majority; it means always having to say you're sorry.

It has been called 'The Law of Unintended Consequences'; with the fall-out from the Scarman and MacPherson reports still reverberating, it might also be appropriate to consider 'The Law(yer)s of Unintended Consequences'. We have to stand firm against Liberal judges, their ratchet and the politically correct 'Thought Police', rather than slavishly submitting to its prejudices.

While in the countryside, the Women's Institute lay on tea and biscuits for the new immigrant citizens of the United Kingdom and welcome them to their villages and homes: there is no urban equivalent to welcome our rural peasants into the metropolis. Both their dress and demeanour mark them out as dinosaurs on their way to extinction. And there is only embarrassment in the King's Road at their presence. I think to myself: 'Ah, but tomorrow, like Wat Tyler and his hordes, they will deface the streets of London.'

37

March of the Aliens

We get up early on the great day and set off for breakfast, but it is not an auspicious start. As we head towards Hyde Park the streets of Chelsea and Belgravia are disgorging from a thousand expensive apartments and renovated town houses a whole stream, not of shabby aliens from the countryside, but expensive-looking types – businessmen and mortals from the pages of Debrett. The men can be identified as the rich and the aspiring rich by their Jermyn Street shirts and ties, their brown brogues, their smart trousers and tailored jackets from Savile Row. The women, panting like Labradors at their partners' sides, are all kitted out in pseudo Country Casuals that they have purchased in institutions like Holland & Holland. Although you can buy the same kit from Cornwall Farmers in Penzance at a tenth of the price, these good ladies need a Holland & Holland label so that they can hold their heads high in society. Many of them look like those grinning female chimpanzees that you see in adverts for country clothing in *Country Life* and *The Field*. Oh, my God, I think; this march is going to be a dismal failure; a class event.

Our party assembles for breakfast at the Royal Thames Yacht Club as it overlooks the Hyde Park start line. As we eat a delicious breakfast we can see this massive queue stretching right back to the Albert Hall. One elderly lady, so her grandson with his mobile phone informs me, has been up early but she is right back at Knightsbridge Barracks and she is still standing there two hours later. One hour after the designated Start, the massive queue is static. It has not moved at all. So we decide to cheat and gather up the family, including a one-year-old granddaughter in her pram with several other children, and set off under the Hyde Park underpass into Green Park, where we join the march in Piccadilly. However, we have hardly marched half a mile when several members of our entourage insist on taking coffee in Whites Club in St James's, a watering hole of some notoriety.

It is complete bedlam in Whites, full of bawling and whinnying women going yackkety-yak-yackkety-yak. Whites Club is an unusual place in London, where new money and old mix, mainly around the bar.

The bar is a place for bounders. The bar at Whites has ruined more reputations and disseminated more gossip than any other cubbyhole of a similar size in the United Kingdom. This club is the last stop on the way to extinction for public schoolboys, mainly Etonians who have never grown up. Although there is a women's annexe in Whites, women are not part of the place at all, and lucky them. A certain class of husband, or should I say husbands with little class, may have spent half a lifetime, forty years or more, baying and guffawing in Whites, and their wives have never seen the gentlemen's quarters at all. But on this unique occasion wives are welcome, or at least tolerated, in the men's club. They are obviously overcome with emotion at being allowed to see this place where so many of their husbands have drunk and gossiped their life away. The place is absolutely crammed with baying, whinnying, chortling, hee-heeing women from the shires. A secondary excuse for coming into this place is also, of course, to go to the loo. Women are always searching for a 'loo'.

While the members of Whites fight their way to the several bars for gin and tonic and champagne, the women keep up a high-pitched squawking and screeching with a background twitter rather like a flock of starlings. The atmosphere is overwhelming and ghastly so, unable to gather up my women in the crush, I escape for a military reconnaissance to a much more civilised establishment across the road, called Spratts, where I think we might have lunch. But this club, where I am a member, is virtually empty and there is no point in taking my harem there. So all ten of us rejoin the march and have a second halt for a club lunch near Trafalgar Square.

The Leg of Mutton is, in my view, the most civilised club in London, full of intelligent, interesting people, most of whom would never be seen dead in Whites. After a pleasant lunch, the members being especially tolerant and gracious to my granddaughters and their pre-teen cousins, we set off to rejoin the throng for the second time. Here the true glory of the occasion is revealed, as we reinsert ourselves at the top of Whitehall. How can I describe the impact that this huge crowd has upon me? We are told that there are 407,791 marchers – not 407,792, mark my words. In reality, of course, there are well over half a million people from every single walk of life and from every part of the United Kingdom. Thousands of my neighbours from Cornwall left by coach at 3 a.m. and got home at 4 a.m. the next day.

Clearly they have a grievance against this arrogant metropolitan élite that calls itself a government. Hunting is the symbolic issue, but the march is about much more than that. Previous Labour governments had neither the clout nor the guts nor the massive majority to take on their traditional hate figure – the rural Tory voter. It seems extraordinary that any government could succeed in arousing these docile, placid country people from their torpor. Yet by sheer ignorance of the countryside and its ways, the government had succeeded – not that it cares one jot.

The banners held aloft by these people are revealing. 'Help the farmers' plight before we vanish out of sight'; 'Don't care, Mr Blair'. The hunting community is overwhelmingly represented by what Labour would call 'our people' – the working classes. The 'Heather Lurcher Club', 'The Celtic Bloodhounds', 'The Dove Valley Mink Hounds', 'The Ludlow Hunt Pony Club', 'The Wigtown Bay Wild Fowlers'. I have never seen such a wonderful cross-section of incomes, backgrounds and occupations in one place before. But the overwhelming impression is of very ordinary country people who have had enough of these regulating bureaucratic busybodies in Whitehall.

It is extraordinary how urban and suburban people think of a countryside riven with class distinctions. The chattering classes play this tune because it is fun to write about dissolute aristocrats, crusty retired colonels and hunt balls in country mansions; it appeals to metropolitan prejudices. In fact, apart from the rich businessman immigrant to the countryside, who keeps himself to himself, all country people share in the problems of closures of rural post offices, inadequate public transport, crippling petrol costs, diminishing village stores and high community taxes. That is why five hundred thousand people came, and I doubt if there are a thousand rich among them.

It is a patriotic gathering too. The Union Jacks are mixed with the flags of St George, St David, St Andrew, St Patrick and St Pirren. There is a sense of outrage that Blair has surrendered to his backbench hooligans who want to ban the traditional sport of country people but there is also the underlying feeling that this same metropolitan élite would sell our country down the river to France and Germany and their bureaucratic allies in Brussels. It is a great day and would warm the heart of any Englishman. Somehow we will all prevail.

38

fish-heads in Shepherd's Bush

I set off for Shepherd's Bush to see William's office; William is my second son, and he has started a pop music publishing business after cutting his entrepreneurial teeth selling second-hand trainers (the dirtier the better) to the French in Paris. Originally he was in Soho but he moved to Shepherd's Bush to cut the rent. Chris, his only helper, who is the son of a bookshop owner in Oxford, meets me at the Underground because he says I will never find the office. He is right. Chris leads me across the road and we plunge into the Shepherd's Bush market, along the railway arches, past an Islamic fundamentalist bookshop, and then up two flights of rickety stairs much obstructed by packing cases and every other kind of impedimenta.

At the top there is a large, bright, white-painted attic with dormer windows. At one end are William's friends, Renshaw and Heime, who run their own architectural business. William has the other end, filled by stacks of CDs, computers and speakers, but comfortably bright and cheer-ful. I am impressed. William is trying to sell one of his record labels, called Inertia – an appropriate name for his very modern, laid-back approach to life and business. At the moment he has an auction going with the major record companies, so he may be on to a good thing.

After chatting to Chris and William's two friends, who are coming to Cornwall in the autumn to shoot partridges on our farm, I am advised to browse through the market. This is a real education. It is almost impossible to believe that places like this exist in England. But they do, and are entirely typical of modern Britain. The atmosphere is like a bazaar in Bombay or Karachi. I seldom see a white face and the stalls are all owned by an assortment of Pakistanis, Indians and Jamaicans – there are also many Afghan, North African and Turkish immigrants in Shepherd's Bush. I am struck by how good-looking all the girls seem to be. They are so welcoming and friendly, with a totally uninhibited approach to their customers.

Alongside the Kenya Halal Meat and Poultry Butchers and the Medina Butchers, there is a fresh fish stall selling every kind of fish at knock-down prices. I notice that the heads and tails of the fish have all been cut off and, just round the corner, there is another stall of blackened – presumably smoked – dried fish-heads and tails in great tubs. The vegetable stalls are piled high with yam and sweet cassava, eddoes and Ghana cocoa yam. Huge mangoes are selling at 60p (in Safeway in Chelsea they are £1.40). The avocados are half the price of the supermarket offerings, as are all the vegetables. The atmosphere in Shepherd's Bush market couldn't be more friendly and relaxed.

I spend some time in a little shop that is wholly dedicated to Ethiopian memorabilia. There are videos of the history of Ethiopia and a great deal of literature and film about Haile Selassie, the Lion of Judah. Haile Selassie is revered as a saint and the founder of their religion by the Rastafarians.

A beautiful girl – the Ethiopians and Somalis are surely among the most striking people in the world – tells me that she gives the proceeds of her video sales to help the starving people in Ethiopia. I don't know; it is a good sales pitch. She was clearly born in this country, but she says her great ambition is to visit the birthplace of her parents and her ancestors. I fall in love with her immediately and have to leave her shop with haste.

Connected with the history and culture of Ethiopia, I come across the Rasta Community Centre and the Rasta Café. The Rastas gather there all day to smoke ganja, drink beer and play pool; the sweet smell of ganja wafts out of the Community Centre into the adjoining area.

Near the Rastas' place, to be recycled as an 'Executive Club Lounge' (a British Airways initiative, like the London Eye), there is the Eritrean Community Centre. Unlike the Rastas, the Eritreans have ambition, but through no fault of their own they are mostly jobless. Although they spend much of their time watching videos of 'explosions', they attend English language lessons in the afternoon. Rumour has it that British Telecom is planning to privatise Directory Enquiries and I am considering setting up an Eritrean 'call centre' to keep this vital function here in England. While it is easier to understand 'English as she is spoken' in Bombay and Manila than the patois spoken in Glasgow and Belfast, we must try and recover more of

these 'call centres' back to our own country where hopefully some of the employees can find England on a map.
I can't really remember how it was possible to exist before
'Customer Services' were available to help us out of our
difficulties.

I shall be speaking to Barclays, my former bankers,
various insurance companies, South West Water and
Electricity, British Gas, BT and the London Electricity
Board who all find their customers an infernal nuisance
to see if they can switch their customers to the Eritrean
call centre (which initially at least, will be located in
Hammersmith with only a branch 'Customer Services'
operation in Asmara on the Red Sea).

I am told that this interesting corner of London is under
the control and administration of Bert, a chainsmoker and a
man of considerable character, aged over seventy, who has an
eighteen-year-old Colombian girlfriend; there is a picture of
her on his desk. He has several kids but no wife and spends
much of his time when he is not in the market travelling to
exotic destinations with his girlfriend. Perhaps I will meet
him on my Viking cruise. He welcomed William and his
friends when they took their premises with the comment:
'We can do with a bit of posh around here.'

Bert has an 'enforcer' called Charlie. Charlie is a large
Jamaican muscleman – some say he has three bullet holes
in his chest. He drives around in a big Mercedes blasting
out a mixture of military music and Beethoven and by all
accounts is very charming, except when he goes about the
business of repossession and confiscation.

William tells me that he and his friends frequently lunch

nearby at the Blue Café on the Uxbridge Road. It is run by an Englishman who seems to have a coterie of young Thai girls, who cook and work at the back of the premises. Chris says that although the café is in dire need of refurbishment, the Thai curries are delicious – £5 for a curry or £5.60 with a bottle of water.

As I am gazing at a shop called Doo Grow – 'help for hair that won't grow' – completely hung about with wigs and potions, a Sainsbury's shopping trolley is pushed by stacked with beef, chicken and, did I see, pigs' trotters? Surely not. On the top of this barrow of uncooked meat there seems to be a pile of skinned monkeys – imported bushmeat from Africa being in great demand and selling at very high prices in Shepherd's Bush Market.

As I move back on to the Shepherd's Bush Road, I pass a tailor called Segena De Tailor and on an adjoining stall is a row of 'ladies' full-sized briefs', which are clearly designed with the 'bigger lady' in mind. I find the whole place fascinating, friendly and utterly bewildering in the sense that I have stumbled upon an Asian-Caribbean country in the midst of London.

I then retreat to Hammersmith because I have set my mind on visiting the Hammersmith Palais, in my youth possibly the most famous dance hall in all of London. A Mr Wonderful tea dance is in progress, but the place is now called not the Hammersmith Palais but Po Na Na. Po Na Na is evidently a Moroccan company and is famous for its Saturday night 'school discos', to be found on www.schooldisco.com. There is a long waiting list to get into these fancy dress evenings and you have to book ahead. Everyone dresses up – men and women – in school uniform; all the girls dig out their comprehensive school uniforms and on Saturday night all the surrounding bars in Hammersmith are crammed with people in school uniforms getting absolutely sloshed.

As I enter, Mr Wonderful is announcing: 'We are short of men today. Michael, can you dance with two women?' I sit in a corner and chat to a man of seventy-four who says he remembers 'when this place had two huge bands on a revolving stage and one of the principal bandleaders was Joe Loss'. Now it is a very run-down hall with these famous Saturday discos in the evenings. But Mr Wonderful holds his tea dances here once a month; I fear that it is a very pale version of what I have attended in Battersea, Dartford and Bromley.

Hammersmith is simply packed with people, people from every country in the world. The huge crowds parading the streets remind me of Beijing in the summer months, a place where you are left in no doubt that you are walking in the capital city of the most populous nation on the earth.

Tory delegate who bought Edwina Currie's
memoirs at the Conservative Conference

39

The Conservative Party Conference

In *Here Today, Gone Tomorrow*, the bestselling saga of my short political career, now in paperback, I tell the story of the Conservative Party Conference in Bournemouth in 1983. The title of the book came about following my walk-out during an interview with Robin Day, when he was kind enough to suggest that all politicians are here today but gone tomorrow. It was a perfectly fair comment for him to make but it was said in an aggressive way as part of his effort to recapture the initiative in what is the endless, boring verbal fencing still used nowadays by political interviewers; they think it clever.

Here I am, on my way to Bournemouth for the Conservative Party Conference. I must be mad. Why am I going to this bear garden when a whole twenty years ago I described the conference as 'the annual low point of my political year'? The truth must be told. I am hoping to sell and autograph the few remaining copies of my memoir. This will be done at the Politico's bookstall. Frankly it is a perfectly pointless journey, because after everyone in the printing, publication and distribution business has ripped me off I am left with about £1 for each copy sold. It is unlikely that I will sell sufficient copies to cover the cost of my fare.

I join the ticket queue in Waterloo behind a very distinguished elderly parson with a stick. I reckon he must be even older than me. When he reaches the friendly ticket man behind his bullet-proof window, my elderly friend shouts at the top of his voice, 'One old man's return to Bournemouth with two Freedom Passes please.' I am amazed. I always carry a card called a Senior Rail Card. In other words, 'I am a doddering old bugger and I want a cheap fare.' But what was the second Freedom Pass? I do not know. It turns out to be my bus pass, which Mr Livingstone, the Mayor of London, grants me for being geriatric, devastated by poverty, disabled and troubled by every other kind of problem which afflicts the old. So when I reach the bullet-proof window, I say to the helpful ticket man behind his emplacement, 'Can I show my bus pass *and* my Senior Rail Card?' 'Oh, yes,' he says, 'if you have a bus pass you pay £5 less on all the trains.'

Sitting on the train to Bournemouth opposite me is a young mum with her five-year-old boy. The boy has irrepressible energy, which in the early part of the journey puts his mum in an increasing rage. 'Stop it, stop it, stop it,' she says at least thirty times. Slap, slap, 'stop it, stop it', slap, slap. I call the guard and say that the good lady is breaking the European Union guidance code on how to discipline young children – nowadays, according to the European Union, you are not allowed to slap your children. The guard seems uninterested in the European

Union, although he does pull out of his satchel the European Union code on 'How to act in an emergency'.

When the mum rises from her seat to take the young lad to the loo I estimate her weight at something over 14 stone. She wears a white singlet and her bra straps are her most noticeable fashion accessory. I remember reading that Serena Rees, who established Agent Provocateur in 1994, took exception to 'the dirty grey straps under vest tops seen all summer on the tube' and that had led her to the introduction of her velvet bras with diamante straps in her summer ranges. This mum's trousers are a sort of nylon track suit.

As she leans forward to chastise her son, her ample waist bulges out of her bare midriff and she reveals a sort of G-string. As the journey wears on she gets more and more impatient with her irrepressible son. 'Stop it, stop it' rings through the carriage. The little boy takes no notice whatsoever. I mark him out as a future prime minister or at least a general. Less likely, but always possible, he'll grow up to become a permanent resident of Cell 463 in Pentonville. The little brat obviously needs a father to knock him into shape, European Codes or no, but there seems little evidence of one. Poor girl, poor brat – it need not be like this.

Hundreds of people get off the train at Bournemouth and I notice that I am the only one of the train passengers to take a bus (80p). All the other young MPs, advisers, journalists and other Conference riff-raff take a taxi (£3.50). I show my Freedom Pass to the driver of the Bournemouth bus and he snorts in contempt. 'We don't take them here in Bournemouth,' he says. I should add that on the train, waiting to find my final station, I had noticed that the stop before Bournemouth is called Pokesdown. It seems an appropriate name for the bonking Tories attending the Conference, and an encouragement for them to slip across the hotel passage to spend an illicit evening in the arms of the Branch Treasurer.

I make a brief visit to the Conference Hall to sniff the atmosphere. Nothing has changed in twenty years except that the audience seems much younger. They are the same interested, sober citizens who give their free time to church, good deeds, local politics and the Conservative Party.

I am told that the young organisers have reserved all the front seats for people under thirty – 'I'm sorry, Madam, you can't sit here, you are obviously not under thirty' – and instead of the Conference starting at a sensible hour it now all begins at 2.45 in the afternoon – the idea evidently being to catch the media for the evening news. Any young fogies in pinstripe suits are immediately ushered to seats at the back of the hall; jeans, sweatshirts and earrings are all the rage among the organisers.

These organisers have also put up a huge photograph across the whole of the wall behind the speaker with an emaciated open hand begging under a large caption which says, 'It's time to help the vulnerable'. Given that the hall contains thousands of members of the Women's Institute, who spend their lives doling out soup to the poor and needy, it is an ignorant impertinence for these PR trendies who organise the Conference to patronise their elders.

It makes me wonder why the current fashion among the leadership is to fashion the Conservative Party as a 'nice' party.

I do not understand it. We need to appear competent and aware but that does not mean surrender to the latest focus group. It is this political death wish to be liked and to smother people with your concern for their welfare – poverty and misfortune is not their fault, it is 'ours'. If the Conservative Party wants to be the party of the poor and needy, what is it trying to conserve? What is the point of being a Conservative unless your foremost loyalty is to the struggling independent-minded middle classes? It is partly the fault of the self-indulgent Portillo and his mistaken acolyte Francis Maude. Why be bludgeoned into following these 'modernisers' with their intellectual arrogance and supercilious smiles? What does 'modernisation' mean; they never define it.

There is also a big notice advertising the Conference Ball: 'To celebrate the fifty-year reign of Her Majesty The Queen. Tickets £15.' Why here? There is another notice saying, 'Do not miss the event, the chances are that you will buy a raffle ticket and attain a weekend in Gibraltar.' I can't imagine anything worse. 'First prize – one weekend in Gibraltar; second prize – two weekends in Gibraltar.'

I nearly stay for the ball to demonstrate my dancing skills, but I would be the only ageing gigolo there. It is now the girls who issue invitations, not the men, and I would be a wallflower waiting hopelessly for invitations. I also miss the Conference Dinner, advertised with the attractive notion that 'each table will be chaired by a celebrity from show business, sport or the arts'. God! What fun, sitting next door to a 'celebrity'!

We then have a speech about creating opportunities 'for the over-fifties'. Thank you very much. This is followed by a tedious and patronising lecture from the chairman of the Council of One-Parent Families, who implies, quite correctly, that the audience is not particularly sympathetic to her cause. Have the organisers of this Conference gone completely bonkers? This, like every other Conference before it, is a social occasion for the delegates to meet their friends and exchange experiences. If the so-called modernisers prostrate themselves to media requirements, the media will do them in. The threat to the new Conservative Party is pretending to be what it is not. It is all about these pathetic 'focus groups' which spell ruin.

I then repair to the Politico's bookstall, the reason for my journey. It is completely monopolised by a totally frenetic Ann Widdecombe, who is selling her new novel, *An Act of Treachery*. Her chin hardly appears above the pile of books in front of her but she keeps up a completely inane torrent of sales patter; as she brandishes a copy she shrieks, 'No sex. No violence. No swearing.' I have heard and seen it all before from banana salesmen in the Caledonian Market. Is Ann the offspring of an East End trader? I watch her performance with amazement, mainly because it seems to me to lack any dignity, and I think to myself, why is it that I did not encounter this good lady when I was in the City? I could have recruited her as a bond salesman in the futures market, where I would have dressed her in a colour-ful jacket and she could gesticulate and shout all day long.

Next to Ann Widdecombe is Matthew Parris, flogging his recent memoir. It is therefore with trepidation and a sense of utter inadequacy that I join these two celebrities as an ex-MP that no one has heard about for twenty years. I whisper to Matthew Parris that, although I think that Ann is very odd and her views on everything hopelessly mistaken, I wonder why is she not being used. Surely she has the talent and experience that the Tory opposition needs. She has exactly the same urge for self-publicity as that other famous Tory lady, Edwina Currie.

I have to say that as I stand with Matthew Parris and Ann Widdecombe, waiting to sign my book, I notice that the shelf behind me is entirely taken up with copies of Edwina Currie's diaries. Initially people look at me, then past me at Edwina, cast their eyes to the ground and walk away. It is Edwina Currie's fault that I only sell ten books. Another Bateman cartoon is in the making, with a shame-faced Tory delegate buying a book; underneath the caption says: 'The Tory delegate who bought Edwina Currie's diaries at the Conservative Conference.' I could not detect any sense that people thought better or worse of Edwina's lover. No one really cared. Like me, Edwina and her lover are part of history. *Now* is all that matters.

Well, what do I think of it all? It is completely ghastly. It is the crowds. The endless pitter-patter of feet as hundreds of sweaty delegates move in circles around the Conference Hall and its displays. Rather like those scenes you see on television of the hajj, with Muslim faithful going round and round the Kaaba. The adoration of the Conference crowds has always been the same. Nothing daunts them. Can I say funny things about them? It would be easy to be cynical, but in fact they are the salt of the earth, the very heart and foundation of our country. One day this country will belong to them again.

40

All-Day Breakfast

I t may be quite a weekend. I travel down to Cornwall by train and am met by my admirable farm manager, Tony Farnaby. 'Are we ready for the invasion?' I ask. 'Yes,' he thinks. 'There are plenty of partridges and pheasants on the farm and Mandy has prepared the cottages.'

It is William's shooting weekend when he invites his friends to stay. They are a delightful lot but quite eclectic; about as different from a conventional team of shooting folk as you can possibly imagine. There is Ben, who has his own record company like my son. There is Renshaw, the architect who shares an office in Shepherd's Bush with William. His partner, Heime, is also coming. There is James, an insurance broker in a special corner of the market, and Tony, the son of a famous comedian, who is married to an Italian girl.

A number of other girls will also appear but where they will sleep and with whom remains uncertain until they put in a late appearance. Mandy has some problem in making up the beds, for it is impossible to predict who will occupy the double beds and who the single beds. Millie, William's girlfriend, is also coming and she will do the cooking.

'Is Millie bringing all the food?' I ask. 'This is your party but have you got enough for two breakfasts, one shooting lunch and a big dinner on the Saturday evening?' 'Don't worry,' says William, 'it is all organised.' If it is organised, I think, it will be a miracle. William is the most horizontal, most laid-back individual that I have ever met. How can my own son be so relaxed? I am never relaxed. If we are giving a dinner party or we have guests to stay, I am in a frightful dither for days on end but nothing, absolutely nothing, ruffles my younger son.

'I tell you what,' I say, 'if Millie does not bring enough food we can open some packing cases of All-Day Breakfast.' 'You must be crazy,' he replies. 'I am not giving expired tins of All-Day Breakfast to my friends.' 'Why not?' I ask. 'All-Day Breakfast is a real canned delicacy.' He laughs. 'It is made up of baked beans, chopped-up bacon and artificial eggs.' 'The eggs are not artificial,' I protest. 'They are scotch eggs, floating among the tomato sauce and beans and, in any event, you should know that Smedley's All-Day Breakfast is one of Tesco's most successful product lines.'

I came by these packing cases in the following way. I became convinced that on 1 January 2000 the whole distribution and logistical system of the country would collapse as we entered the new millennium. I was still, at that time, the chairman of the largest canning business in Europe so I ordered for myself, at wholesale prices, enough tinned food to feed my family for at least three months. In our cellar there are packing cases of mushrooms, peas, kidney beans, rhubarb, gooseberries, tomatoes, tinned fruit salad and, of course, All-Day Breakfast, all stacked away. I often suggest that we open a can or two but my daughter in particular thinks it very funny. 'How can we eat out of these dreadful tins?' she says. 'They are all time-expired.'

I reply that 'time-expired' on cans is just a marketing gimmick. 'A can of food will last for fifty years if necessary. During the war we had packing cases of food stacked away in the attic of my school in case of an invasion by the Nazis. 'You simply don't understand,' I add, 'that it is essential always to have available emergency supplies of food.' At school in 1945–7, I tell her, I was absolutely starving. I swore that I would never be caught short of food again so 'I never go anywhere without some emergency rations in my pocket'. The children think I'm mad. 'What are the supermarkets for?' they say. I fear that they will find out one day that in an emergency the supermarkets will have nothing on their shelves at all.

As I have not been in Cornwall for several weeks, I had plugged in my electric blanket and set off from home for the railway station to meet my son. When we arrive back at the house, some thirty minutes later, there is a strong pungent smell throughout the house. 'Something's on fire,' says William. Indeed it is. My bed is on fire. I rush off for the fire extinguisher, which belches powder around the room, but the mattress goes on smouldering. So we manhandle it with difficulty into the back yard and douse it with water.

So I have no bed. Where am I to sleep? The bedrooms have all been prepared for guests. I telephone my daughter-in-law and ask if I can use her cottage which adjoins the house. 'Of course,' she says. That night it is bitterly cold in the cottage and I cannot sleep. William drives the white van to Newquay to pick up Kate from the local airport. I awake at midnight and there is no sign of the white van. Oh, my God, I think, I have lost my white van and the chicken stock is on the Aga and it will boil the saucepan dry. So I rush out of the cottage, nearly starkers, to move the saucepan off the stove. At two o'clock I wake again. There is still no white van in the courtyard so once again I go in search of my son, fearing that he has had an accident. It is bitterly cold and I am in nothing more than my nightshirt. After quite a search I find eight of William's guests drinking in another cottage and the van stands there outside in perfect peace and harmony. I could not bear to lose my white van.

The next morning I have organised the beaters for half past nine. All William's guests have been up till four o'clock playing cards and drinking in the cottages. At nine o'clock I am getting desperate. I have to get them out of bed to save my embarrassment with the beaters. Eventually the party is assembled and we move off at ten o'clock. We shoot ten partridges, forty pheasants and put up at least fifteen woodcock. None is shot, I'm rather glad to say.

Another of William's friends is called Simon. He was at school with William. Simon's presence at this shooting weekend reminds me that I have only once been on the front pages of the tabloids. At school William and his friends were in the habit of climbing out of their rooms and making their way to a private house in Windsor where they provided late-night entertainment for the girls from a local convent. It was all quite innocent, or so I'm told. These late-night parties were rudely interrupted when one of the parents discovered his daughter's late-night antics and reported the matter in a fury to the headmaster of William's school. There was a frightful fuss and the boys were gated, sent home early for the holidays.

The next day the front page of the *Sun* only had one leading story under an enormous headline. I was sitting on the front bench in the House of Commons and noticed a policeman beckoning me from behind the Speaker's chair. 'Have you seen the *Sun*, sir?' he said. 'Oh, my God,' I replied. 'Am I in it?' 'Yes,' he said, smiling broadly. Placing his hand upon the headline, I read 'SEX BAN ON NOTT'. The policeman's thumb was covering the word SON. The title was 'SEX BAN ON NOTT'S SON' and that was the policeman's form of humour. Very funny. This headline, of course, provoked the country's leading scandal sheet, the *Daily Mail*, to launch a tirade against this famous school for punishing boys by sending them back early for their holidays. We were not popular in the school.

41

Off to Norway – at last!

Winston is late; he is always late for our minicab journeys to Heathrow. We are due to catch Scandinavian Airlines flight number 560 to Copenhagen and onwards to Bergen for our Norwegian cruise. We do not wish to miss the flight but have to accept that Winston, our temporary chauffeur, is not an early riser. Winston is black. He is monosyllabic but he has a sweet smile and a very delightful personality; nothing seems to ruffle him.

'How many children do you have?' we ask Winston in the car. 'Five,' he replies and volunteers the information that he was born in the Congo. 'I send my children back to the Congo for their education,' he says. 'England is not a good place for schooling. The discipline and moral standards in the schools are much higher in the Congo than here in England. All my friends send their children out of England so that they can get a proper education.'

I think to myself that when New Labour's passion for social engineering has successfully shut down our ancient universities to the 'brightest and best' young students in the country, they will still be able to obtain their degrees at the University of Kinshasa. Why should the middle classes complain, when their children can obtain a broad-based education in the Congo rather than at Oxbridge?

Winston drives a smart, nearly new and clean Mercedes. It is much cleaner than our Mercedes and it smells good. Admittedly when we drive our car from our farm in Cornwall to London it carries potatoes, chicken fertiliser for the garden in Chelsea and pheasants for the deep freeze – so the car is something of a tip. Winston's Mercedes only carries human cargo.

My wife and I speculate on how Winston has become so wealthy, and decide that the real disposable income in Brixton, where he lives, is higher than in Chelsea. It is an entrepreneurial society generating a lot of 'new money' from barter and trade in stolen goods and substances. It escapes the predations of the taxman, who removes half of everything we earn in Chelsea, but Brixton sensibly subscribes to the black economy, hence its vibrant character.

Yes, we are to go on a cruise – our first. Experience of life has taught me the foolishness of ever making any decision of importance about the future; events always intervene to render any decision absolutely pointless. It is an excellent rule in politics never to take a decision. Only fools lacking political ambition take decisions. The route to high office as a minister and to the admiration of one's peers is to avoid decisions at all costs. Decisions only lead you into trouble. Call a meeting. Set up a committee. Find a long-winded elderly lawyer (not difficult) as chairman. Encourage it to be thorough but ambiguous in its conclusions. Five years later, when it reports, withdraw the paper for consideration and lose it in the civil service files.

On no account allow a committee to report in less than three years – or people will remember why it was appointed in the first place.

While hijacking any decisions it is nonetheless vital to give an impression of perpetual motion – ceaseless activity. This is achieved by announcing a stream of 'initiatives'. Initiating and targeting, modernising, reforming, planning, launching and relaunching all require press announcements. Initiatives are quite different from decisions: they lead nowhere. Decisions have a cost.

When I was a Trade Secretary, I announced on 20 August 1979 a 'Burn a Form a Day' campaign. I had discovered that the Board of Trade boasted over five hundred separate forms for compilation by hapless British business. My initiative dominated the headlines for forty-eight hours. The number of forms continued to rise and Trade now boosts over a thousand forms but my initiative was an undoubted success.

How have things changed in the political life of modern Britain? Just as I have noted developments in our spiritual life so I have to identify recent trends in government. Walter Bagehot's seminal work *The English Constitution* was written in 1867 and it may be in need of substantial revision.

Indeed; things have moved on since I was in government in 1979. Now ministers are forbidden to take initiatives. All initiatives are reserved for the Prime Minister himself. Ministers have become what Bagehot described as the 'dignified' part of the Constitution, together with the monarchy and Parliament. Ministers and Parliament no longer matter.

A schedule of forthcoming initiatives is drawn up weekly for the Prime Minister by the Department of Public Relations under two aristocrats, Lord Tim Bell and Lady Carla Powell, who pass their recommendations to No. 10. This is the tactical arm of the government.

The strategic arm of government which conducts 'blue skies thinking' is under the control of another aristocrat, a businessman with experience of running a slim, efficient, commercial enterprise – he is Lord John Birt, formerly of the BBC. Other advisers joining the presidential suite, all with desks at No. 10, known 'thinkers' with strong ethnic credentials, are Madonna, Ali G, Steve Coogan and Geri Halliwell. No one quite knows what they think about but the announcement of their appointment was met with universal acclaim.

Given my observant nature and long experience and knowledge of government, I have been invited by advisers at No. 10 to plan, reform, modernise, edit and relaunch *The English Constitution* by Bagehot so that it is available with the other list of government achievements at the next General Election – that is if the British Constitution still exists in a few years' time.

I don't really want to go on the cruise – the decision to do so was a mistake. But I have many weaknesses, one of the least offensive being that I cannot resist a bargain. Because of September 11, the Americans have cancelled their cruises, so the Norwegians have slashed their prices and the bargain seems irresistible. The smell of a bargain far outweighs the decision that I would never go on a cruise. However, I intend to make the best of it – and hunt down my Viking heritage.

It bores me even to think of this trip – the organised jollity, the awful intimacy of tablemates, the endless walking round and round because you can't walk anywhere else, the claustrophobia.

We have debated over several months what clothes to take. My wife has said, 'I will need several suitcases to meet every kind of weather from the Arctic autumn to the temperate breezes blowing off the Gulf Stream. More particularly,' she says, 'I will need a different dress each night for the captain's table.' I am instructed to take a dinner jacket but I refuse.

The big issue on this cruise is whether I can control my testosterone for one whole week at sea. It has been bothering me greatly for the past four months or so. Perhaps it is the last blast of the trumpet. My wife was advised by her friend, 'You must lace his coffee with bromide', but it does not seem to have worked. I understand that a famous actress insisted that her fourth husband should visit a sex therapist before she married him. It was part of their pre-nuptial agreement. I have seriously considered visiting a sex therapist myself as I am worried what it will be like on a ship for a whole week cooped up with a group of old age pensioners. Will I emerge from this adventure reinvigorated to face the remaining few years left to me, fishing, shooting, boating and lusting after virgins in the King's Road? Or will I become a cruise junkie, setting off to discover ever-new corners of the Pacific Ocean in the company of an army of American widows?

42

Heathrow: Checking in

On arrival at Heathrow Terminal 3, another multicultural melting pot, we seek out SAS, the Scandinavian Airlines check-in. It passes smoothly but I have been in a nervous state for at least a week because I do not see how our bags can switch over to the Bergen flight in the short transit time allowed at Copenhagen. I ask the check-in girl how our transit in Copenhagen plus our bags could possibly be undertaken in fifty minutes flat. She assures me that there is no problem, so my first excuse for a heart attack at Terminal 3 is aborted.

We then seek out the British Airways lounge. The previous day, in accordance with my earlier (fifty years earlier) military training, I had telephoned Special Services to find out if a Scandinavian Airlines passenger could use a British Airways lounge. Only if you have a Premier or a Gold card they say. I have a Premier card.

These cards are not given to businessmen who spend their lives flying around the world, either on business or as a means of getting away from their wives, but for 'services to British Airways', who treat you or me as a sort of geriatric VIP. Glamorous women greet you with huge smiles and a trolley or a wheelchair as you step off the aeroplane. This privilege remains the only practical residue of a more famous past, when I was whisked to the VIP lounge, which one shared with assorted Arab princes and ambassadors and sometimes with their wives, mistresses and concubines – some of them covered from head to foot in a black gauze sheet.

The memory of it reminds me of a trip to Saudi Arabia. I had expressed the wish to my Saudi host that I might be allowed in my spare moments to visit the royal hawks and camels. In accordance with the courtesy granted to distinguished visitors in Riyadh, I was taken to a compound where all the royal family's hawks were on display and then on to the enclosure to see the royal camels. The royal camels were engaged in hectic copulation and there was a sort of grandstand so that the royal ladies could watch – as they did not have much to do all day. I managed to sneak a peek at the royal ladies and I could not help but notice that the younger and more beautiful ladies were in a state of great excitement as they watched the copulating royal camels – rather more congenial than a copulating Arab, I suppose. It was clear that I was a particularly privileged visitor in this, one of the many palaces of the King.

Now the thing about this Viking saga about to begin is that at my advanced old age I cannot prevent my mind wandering into the experiences of my youth, but I shall try hard, as the cruise approaches, not to be diverted by Saudi Arabian camels or recite an endless range of stories of a misspent youth – many of them experienced as an itinerant international businessman with time on his hands in foreign cities.

Anyhow, we set out to find the haven of the British Airways First Class Lounge which, after walking several miles in the wrong direction, we eventually reach, to spend the intervening two hours. Two hours of totally unnecessary pensioner's padding, as I call it. My wife insists on time to relax – and, of course, to use the loo. While we await the departure of our flight I settle down to read the newspapers, which are still rattling on about Edwina Currie. I want to know whether we are about to go to war with Iraq, but this issue apparently does not merit the interest of the editors.

After an hour or so my wife reminds me that a bottle of wine on board the ship is likely to cost at least £20, Norway being one of the most expensive countries in the world. So I set off to buy some bottles in Duty Free – now called Tax Free, to fleece the unsuspecting alcoholic punter. There I stock up with wine at £5 a bottle, and I also obtain a half bottle of brandy – the tipple much favoured by my glamorous wife. At the check-out a lady says: 'May I see your boarding card, sir?' I show her my boarding card to Copenhagen. 'No, you cannot buy the brandy tax free if you are going to the European Union.' 'I am not going to the European Union,' I say, 'I am merely transiting in Copenhagen. I'm going to Bergen, which due to the wisdom of the Norwegian people is still outside the European Union.' 'That's fine,' she says. 'Show me your Bergen boarding card.' 'I can't,' I reply. 'My Bergen boarding card is in the British Airways lounge.' It was a disastrous mistake leaving my Bergen boarding card behind. I have to pay £12 for the brandy – the outrageous European Union price – instead of £8.50. I set off back to collect my wife in the British Airways lounge.

The arrival of our fellow cruisers on to the SAS flight to Bergen is not auspicious. After all those tea dances I cannot see a single lady whom I would wish to take into my arms for a tango or for a smooching foxtrot. I shall keep my eyes skinned, of course, but it seems that I shall be the youngest passenger on board. The only glamour will be provided by my wife. After forty-three years of marriage her glamour remains undimmed but it can hardly supply that sense of excitement and anticipation that is provided by the chase after a bit of extra-marital flesh.

43

Where is the Captain's Table?

On the bus from Bergen Airport to the boat my wife insists on sitting at the back. I protest that it is right beside the loo. 'Throughout the journey,' I say, 'we will be pestered by a continual stream of pensioners queuing for the loo. I will neither be able to look out of the windows at soggy Bergen – we land in driving rain and fog – nor gain further acquaintance with the passengers as they make a frantic passage to relieve themselves of the SAS orange juice which we have just been given on the flight.'

The lady Führer who ticks us off on her clipboard by the bus shouts out, 'Where is Mr Smith?' No answer. 'You will have to wait,' says the Führer. 'I shall have to go back to the airport and find him. Please be patient.' The thing about pensioners is that they are fundamentally patient people. Their expectations are absolutely zero. Experience of a lifetime teaches them that it is unusual for anything to go smoothly. Anything that does go right is an unexpected bonus. Had we been a bus full of young marrieds on their way to a package holiday, or a group of 18–30s on their way for a disco orgy in Ibiza, the bus would have echoed with expletives and singsongs – 'Why are we waiting?' etc. In contrast, our pensioner colleagues would have been perfectly happy to sit in the bus all night and do nothing except think of England.

We join the boat in pouring rain but MS *Nordkapp* seems substantial enough. We check into our cabin. It is tiny. When the two beds are down off the wall it is hardly wide enough to stand between them. My wife is disappointed: she was expecting space and a double bed. As a matter of principle, if not of comfort, I always prefer to sleep in a double bed, so I retrieve my steps to the purser and ask to see a suite. I look it over. It is a little larger than our appointed cabin, and it has a double bed, but on asking I discover that the doubtful pleasure that my wife will gain by sleeping with her husband will just about double the cost of the entire cruise. In fact, the suite would cost us an extra £1000. It would require the presence of the most expensive tart in history to make it financially worthwhile. So I retrace my steps to Cabin 560, the best to be obtained below a suite. We will be spending the whole week in two single bunks.

Having unpacked our bags – the cupboard being quite inadequate to hold my wife's trousseau – we set off to explore the ship. It is clear that it is more of a working ferry – stopping day and night at thirty-eight ports on the journey – than a cruise liner. The ship is very spacious, with excellent observation lounges, comfortable chairs and sofas, and a cafeteria selling monstrously expensive sandwiches and beer – but no ballroom to be seen. Can it possibly be the case, after all those energetic visits to Bromley, Battersea, Dartford and Hammersmith, that I shall be denied my shipboard ballroom dancing? There is indeed a little stage with a tiny wooden floor, room for two or three couples to smooch together (Annabels), but decidedly inadequate to rumba, tango, waltz and foxtrot or anything else remotely energetic for that matter. Entertainment is advertised for the next two nights, with a young male crooner from Warrington – and there is no bridge club.

They say a drowning man sees his whole life flash before him as he breathes his last. It is nothing beside the sense of horror that pervades my whole being when I remember the embarrassment and cost of all those journeys to the suburbs, those cups of tea in civic centres, the KitKats, the communications with Mr Wonderful, the difficulty of dancing with Pearl (seventy-nine) and the rebuke from Jane over my 'one-step' that 'went out in the 1920s'. The pleasure of talking to all my fellow senior citizens at those tea dances is quite forgotten beside the great sense of betrayal – even treachery – that has denied a ballroom to the pensioners on a Norwegian coastal cruise. No ballroom on a cruise. It is unthinkable. What are all us pensioners going to do each evening – gaze at the view and just talk to one another?

I shall have to write a letter to the Queen – no, to the King of Norway – saying that I have a family connection (Viking) with his Royal House and he must put it right at once.

Then what about the mental torture that I endured over a whole weekend of learning bridge with a Tory MP? The pain and embarrassment of being the thickest student at the Julian Dobson Bridge Club? Was it all to be for nought? No bridge on a cruise. It is outrageous. I shall have to write a letter to Omar Sharif, but I am not sure whether he is still with us on this perilous journey through life.

At 2000 hours sharp the doors of the dining room are opened and we go inside full of expectation to seek out the captain's table. There is no captain's table. The captain and his crew are so busy docking, loading and unloading and sailing their supply ferry that they have no time to fraternise. We never see the captain or any of his fellow officers in the dining room. My wife's trousseau will have to be buried at sea – or dumped at a charity shop in Trondheim.

44

'Can I borrow your corkscrew?'

We wake up early after a rather interrupted night. The boat docks at Florö at 0215 hours, Måløy at 0430 hours and Torvik at 0730 hours. The passengers above us are clearly too exhausted for marital exercise, but we do hear all sorts of cargo being loaded and unloaded and the bow thrusters make the whole ship shudder as we enter and exit each and every port.

But we go to breakfast full of energy and enthusiasm for our guided tour to the Geiranger Fjord, the Aksla Mountains and the town of Alesund. The breakfast is an excellent buffet, so we steal a collection of biscuits, cheese, fruit and other delicacies and hide them in my wife's handbag so that we do not starve or are bankrupted by paying Norwegian prices on the tour.

On return to the boat in the evening, our first main dinner only provides one incident of any consequence. On the aeroplane to Bergen, SAS had offered us wine for dinner and we kept the quarter bottles, one red and one white, to drink on board. As we approach the dining area carrying these two tiny bottles, a very nice lady, a member

of the crew – acting no doubt for Interpol on behalf of the
Metropolitan Police – says that it is absolutely forbidden to
take wine to the table. 'You must buy off the ship's wine
list,' she says. I am already aware that the cheapest bottle of
wine on board – wine that would not even have come up to
the minimum standard required at a Conservative Wine &
Cheese, costs £23 a bottle. It is out of the question. I am
really quite well off. My income is something in excess of
New Labour's newly introduced minimum wage, but I will
not pay too much for a bottle of wine (or for a double bed).

Undeterred by the solemn warning from the Norwegian
member of the crew, I nonetheless smuggle our two little
bottles in to dinner. While no waitress is looking, I fill our
glasses with the wine and hide the two empty bottles under
the table. When in animated conversation with my wife about
double beds or some such subject, I sweep my arm across the
table and spill my wine all over it. I could have wept. It is all
very well being a criminal if you go undetected, but to lose
the proceeds of the crime by negligence is all too much.

I share my wife's wine glass but this experience reminds
me of a major dilemma. We have four bottles of Heathrow
wine in our cabin, but no corkscrew. On visiting the suite
I had searched it for a corkscrew but the wine in the suite
refrigerator all had screw tops and no corkscrew was to be
found. The stops at each Norwegian port are unlikely to be
sufficiently extended to provide time to find a simple
corkscrew. What is to be done? I say to my wife: 'I must
approach a waitress.' She is appalled. 'It is all very well
being a criminal pensioner but to join a Norwegian waitress as an accessory to the crime is far too much,' she says.

I suppose that I have survived forty-three years of marriage because just occasionally I establish my independence of thought and action by taking not a blind bit of notice of a marital instruction. I therefore approach the stoutest, oldest waitress that I can see, switch on what miniscule charm I can muster and plead with her for the loan of her corkscrew. She looks at me as if I am completely daft. She has years of experience of dealing with geriatric English travellers but this is a new one. 'Can I borrow your corkscrew?' It sounds like an invitation from a teenage female raver in an Ibiza disco to her male partner. I decide that the only hope is to come clean. I plead that I am quite elderly and 'cannot survive without my medicinal non-alcoholic wine, which is in a bottle in my cabin'. I can see her natural Norwegian suspicion melting and a look of sympathy spreading across her chummy face. She takes pity on me. 'You can borrow my corkscrew,' she says, 'but could you return it in the morning?' So I return to the cabin and pull four corks just enough to enable me to complete the job with finger and thumb at a later date.

45

Bombers over Germany

This afternoon we make a visit to the bridge. I am accompanied by four English pensioners of quality. I ask one man whether this is his first cruise, hoping he would say it was. 'Oh no,' he says, 'my wife and I spend half our year on cruise ships when we are not at home in Brentwood, Essex. My favourite ship is the *Saga Star*. Last year we spent three months afloat and sailed around the world.' 'Weren't you bored?' I say. 'Certainly not,' he replies. 'It was wonderful.'

On our visit to the bridge one elderly gentleman asks if the ship has 82S. The captain looks very puzzled; he has never heard of it. 'It is the radar system that we used during the Second World War,' our pensioner says. 'No,' replies the captain, 'the radar system on the ship is not similar to the technology used in the Second World War.' 'Well,' says our friend, 'I was a member of a bombing crew and we made twenty sorties in our Lancasters and Wellingtons over Germany. It is just good luck that I'm still alive.' Everyone nods in agreement.

Our bomber friend then explains patiently to the

captain all the other wizardry that guided the bombing crews over Germany during the Second World War. Then he adds: 'We were flying at several hundred miles an hour, fixing our position every few minutes as we flew. The equipment had to react so quickly because of our speed. I imagine,' he says, 'that our ship, which is cruising at fifteen knots, does not need to use the same equipment that we had over Germany in 1944.' No, the captain thinks not. 'Position-fixing is not quite the same today as in the Second World War.' 'Yes,' I chip in, 'I have a hand-held position fixer that cost me £200 which I use on *Forget-me-Not III*, and I nearly brought it with me to give you a hand.' The captain smiles very sweetly, as if to suggest that the English pensioners are the most eccentric passengers on every cruise.

Although our ship has an eclectic mixture of nationalities – Norwegians, Danes, Dutch, though no Germans that I can find – it is the English lot that I find most interesting. Without exception they appear to represent the prosperous, retired middle classes of England – people like ourselves. They seem well off and as far as I can judge they are enjoying their lifetime savings. I guess that the majority have been self-employed and are readers of the *Daily Telegraph*. There is a smattering of widows travelling with their friends, but the garrulous typecast American widow seems to be absent. Maybe it is September 11 that explains her absence. And still there is no ballroom dancing.

Looking around my fellow English passengers, I am reminded of my constituency supporters when I was in

Parliament; a more loyal, balanced, welcoming, enthusiastic team of elderly people it is impossible to imagine. Why anybody should think that the younger generation of today can be tempted to show an interest in politics I cannot think.

When I was young, the Young Conservatives provided a ready means of meeting the young ladies of the town. Teenagers learned about their impulses and explored one of life's conundrums – why some people appeal and some don't. The handsome one who appeals to all the girls something rotten has the physical dexterity of a carthorse, while the chubby one with acne has a really sensuous rhythm. You did not join the Young Conservatives to indulge in politics: you did so to hunt down a girl. When discos came along and clubbing, fortified by the pill, was everywhere available, the Young Conservatives had nothing left to offer.

*My hat creates mayhem, it seems to have an insatiable
desire to foment trouble at airports and in shops.*

46

Prince Charles's Hat

By this time we are on our fourth day, and are due to arrive at Trondheim at 0815 hours. We have been given a whole four hours of day release from our floating prison – I feel just like Jeffrey Archer.

It is 3 October and as far as the inhabitants are concerned winter has already arrived. The girls in the streets are attractively wrapped in woolly hats, boots and colourful parkas. Hibernation is already setting in. The weather is good and there is a definite nip in the air.

I've always had a secret passion for Norwegian women. After all, they are my distant Viking cousins. I have to admit that on youthful visits to New York, I got to know a Norwegian girl of relatively easy virtue, who was always available when I came to town. She was tall and stately, and I remember her best, apart from her exceptional beauty, for the fact that every time I took her out to dinner she always ordered steak tartare. She used to wear a sort of artificial leather top, actually made of some acrylic substance, which I found particularly stimulating, and when we moved on to one of New York's many

discos, she took it off to reveal a transparent blouse. She
never wore a bra.

Anyhow, we visit the shops in Trondheim. It is a relief
to get ashore. In every shop we are met with friendliness
and perfect English, and I can understand how all these
good-looking Norwegian girls want to escape to London
or New York. I can understand too the frustrations that
Scandinavian women must feel as they anticipate their dark
Arctic winter and the choice between suicide in Stockholm
and a visit overseas. I am told that the young Norwegian
population in America, especially in cities like New
York, greatly exceeds that of their native country, and it
is not surprising. The western world owes everything to
the Scandinavian winter. It drives all these wonderful
Norwegian women out of their beautiful country to stim-
ulate us overseas.

Trondheim is a royal city, capital of the north, with a huge
and rather ugly cathedral used for Norwegian corona-
tions. Interestingly enough, it causes me to reveal a right
royal embarrassment with my hat. I have a flat tweed cap
that I bought at Locks in St James's Street. Inside the hat
under a plastic triangle, no doubt to keep the Brylcreem off
the wool, there are two royal coats of arms and underneath
is writ: 'By Appointment to the Prince of Wales' and on the
other side: 'By Appointment to the Duke of Edinburgh.'

Now this hat has quite extraordinary qualities. For
reasons that are quite unclear there seems to be some device
inserted somewhere in the hat that activates detection
machines all around the world. Those familiar with shopping

in modern emporiums will know that there is a tag attached to clothing which activates an alarm if it passes through two panels at the exit of the shop. The same mechanism exists at airports. My hat seems to have some permanent but completely undetectable tag that creates mayhem with these machines. My hat positively hates them. It is like a cat whose fur rises on its back as soon as it sees a dog approaching.

My problem with this hat is that I forget its almost insatiable desire to foment trouble at airports and in shops. In the winter, when I sometimes wear or carry this hat, it sets off security alarms at Heathrow, Gatwick, Nice and other airports. Going through a process of elimination, electronic engineers and anti-terrorist experts have examined my most intimate private parts and every article of my clothing only to find that the problem arises in my hat. Undoubtedly there is some aggravating substance in the wool; concealed somewhere behind the Prince of Wales or the Duke of Edinburgh there is a problem.

This royal embarrassment seems to be quite unremarkable until my wife suggests that she might have made arrangements to have some bug inserted in my hat so that she can trace my movements. Not unreasonably, she holds me under constant suspicion. I say that it is unlikely 'that if I seek to visit some lady friend in Belgravia I would do so wearing my tweed cap; it is used for shooting and for mucking out our bull shed so it is unlikely to enhance my attractions with a lady friend'.

But my wife's suggestion, made in jest of course, explains the cause of my embarrassment. By some cock-up in Locks of St James's Street I must have bought a hat destined for the Prince of Wales or the Duke of Edinburgh. It is well known that Special Branch's royal protection squad inserts bugs in the hats of the royal family, so that at all times their whereabouts can be traced – a rather inhibiting characteristic of life as a royal and something that caused considerable grief to Princess Diana. Whether this practice results from a private initiative on the part of Special Branch or whether it comes about from requests of the ladies of the royal household anxious to keep tabs on the activities of Prince Charles and the Duke of Edinburgh, I have no means of telling.

This rather long-winded prologue explains why my progress through the quiet and rather empty shops of Trondheim is notable for the alarm created as I pass through the barriers of each and every clothing store. Rather than be arrested and spend my time rotting away in some Viking prison, I throw my hat in front of me through the shrieking barriers to prove my point. Should Locks have made any further hats with similar alarming attributes, I think they should warn the Palace instantly, because none of us would like the suspicion of shoplifting to fall upon the innocent male shoulders of our senior royals. It might be acceptable in some quarters to see Princes Andrew, Edward and Michael locked away, but assuredly we would not wish this to happen to the Duke of Edinburgh or the Prince of Wales.

The day after my return from Norway, I lunched at the Arts Club in Dover Street, a haven of peace and tranquillity. Moreover, as I was in Piccadilly anyhow, I decided to visit Locks in St James's and discuss 'the hat'. I asked them whether they had ever been requested by the Palace to insert a bug so as to trace the whereabouts of erring consorts and princes of the royal blood. No, they said. 'When you bought your hat our electronic debugging machine had gone on the blink. The alarm had been inserted because Guards officers and members of the Court, all customers of Locks, have the habit of walking out without paying their bills, so the bug is inserted to catch them at it. You, sir, must have bought your hat when the debugging mechanism was inoperative'. They apologised, set the machine in motion and by electronic means deactivated the bug directly underneath Prince Charles.

47

'The waitresses descend
like vultures ...'

Tonight we return to dinner with those two quarter
bottles of SAS wine, which we will use to fill our
glasses. I had retreated to the loo and transferred the
Heathrow wine into the quarter bottles, which were then
placed in my wife's handbag. We both change into immaculate evening clothes which we have brought for sitting at
the captain's table, which, as I have already noted, does not
exist. Looking far smarter than any of the other guests, we
enter the dining room and find our table.

There is then an extended pause while the waitresses,
heavily supervised by the head wine waiter, go to every
table to get a wine order. No food is in sight or offered.
The waitresses descend like vultures on the gathered
rotting flesh of a hundred pensioners to take these wine
orders. Morally bludgeoned into looking good, these piti-
ful pensioners order £23 bottles of fourth-rate plonk.
Sitting at tables of ten or more, it is embarrassing for them
to pretend that they cannot afford the wine. The head wine
waiter, aware of peer pressure at each table, exerts maxi-

mum psychological pressure to obtain her orders. Eventually she hoves down on us. I say we are drinking water. She looks at me with a look of utter disdain, almost contempt, and then proceeds to fill the wine glasses on our table with tap water to the brimming top. There is no tumbler or other glass. What are we to do? There is no choice but to gulp down this huge wineglass of water. The eyes of all the waitresses beam down upon us. There is another Bateman carton in this: 'The couple who would not drink wine with their dinner.'

At this stage I decide on a change of tactic. We are being watched. I decide it is impossible to empty the red wine from my wife's handbag into our glasses as it will assuredly be noticed, and we will be led away in front of a hundred or so gawping diners to suffer an indignant lecture from the purser. So we wait until the main course is served; then, placing my wine glass between my legs under the table, I transfer the bottle of white wine from the quarter bottle. I then whisk it up on to the table while my wife keeps lookout – rather like some poor fag doing lookout for an elder boy while he smokes behind the bicycle shed. I then place my glass beside a bunch of flowers so that its yellowish colour will look like a reflection from the flowers. By this time the nervous tension is tremendous and my heart is beating at twice its normal speed. And all my dear wife can say to me is, 'Why are you looking so nervous?'

48

'Alcohol, fighting and women' – Scottish-style

On Thursday morning, our fifth day, we stop at Ornes, by now inside the Arctic Circle about halfway between Trondheim and Tromsö. Each of these marvellous little harbours, with their coloured clapboard houses, seems to be protected from the open sea by islands. What a wonderful place it would be to keep a boat, I think. Hundreds of miles of protected sea, fascinating fjords and inlets everywhere.

As we approached Ornes up another long fjord, the mountains came down to the sea on both sides of us. Along the route, as well as the glaciers in the distance, the high mountains have a dusting of snow. It is so lovely. The lady beside me – a Dane, I think – says to her neighbour: 'I think this is the most beautiful sight that I have ever seen. It makes we want to cry.' She is probably right; day after day we get a most dramatic glimpse of nature in the raw.

As we proceed in the *Nordkapp*, all along the shore we see little farms clinging to the edge of the water, with perhaps five acres of grass, which with twenty-four hours of sunlight produces three cuts of silage for the farm cow and sheep. Each of these farms seems to have a beautiful little boathouse, and I imagine the Vikings setting off to sea.

It is Thursday evening, our fifth, and in spite of all the beauty I realise that I am getting bored with this maritime excursion. Like my Viking ancestors on their little farms, I am ready for some adventure – fighting, pillage and rape. Alas, there is none immediately available, not even ballroom dancing or bridge to keep me out of trouble.

Before returning to my bunk, in a somewhat dejected state, I chat to a friendly couple who come from Glasgow. Suddenly, in conversation, I get carried away by memories of my early youth and my fondness for their Glaswegian cousins, the inhabitants of the Gorbals on the banks of the Clyde. So I tell them a little Scottish tale, which is also in my memoir.

I was eighteen and a young National Service officer serving with the Royal Scots in Berlin. It was a fascinating but divided city in 1951. The Berliners had suffered terrible atrocities at the hands of the conquering Russian soldiers in 1945 but, only six years later, it was already a recovering society, active and pleasure-seeking. Because of the war, the number of German girls greatly exceeded the number of men. The main square outside British military headquarters was known to the men of the Royal Scots as 'Gobbler's Gulch', and the most beautiful young German girls were available for a packet of five Woodbines. We young officers raced sailing dinghies on the Wannsee, took part in all the horse shows and spent several evenings a week on crawls around the proliferating nightclubs, which cost a tax-free half bottle of gin and had all the vulgarity and perversions in which the Germans excel.

But what really endeared the Royal Scots to me was the character of the Scottish soldiers, whom we called the Jocks. The battalion commander, at my request, agreed that I should take my platoon of thirty Scottish soldiers on six-week camp into the Grunewald, the fairly wild park (as it was then) on the banks of the Wannsee.

Isolated as we were from the rest of the Battalion, I got to know the Jocks extremely well. Apart from the NCOs, they were all National Servicemen from Glasgow (although the Royal Scots was an Edinburgh regiment). Most of these young men came from the Gorbals; physically small but wiry and tough, they had an excellent sense of humour but only three consuming interests in life – alcohol, fighting and women.

For the first three days I endeavoured to prevent the faithful band of camp followers (girls from the town) from hanging around the camp perimeter, but since they had every right to be there, there was nothing I could do to drive them away. The situation was made worse by the fact that they found me a source of constant amusement. Discipline was being undermined and the situation was getting out of hand.

I therefore circled the camp with barbed wire and absolutely forbade the men to bring any of these loose women inside the camp perimeter. The sight of their women, however, continued to haunt me (although I must say quite a number of them were agreeably attractive).

About one week after our arrival at this spot I decided to take my jeep out one morning and make a reconnaissance of the edge of the lake in order to find a suitable place to practise a water-crossing exercise. As I did so, I passed a small boathouse and saw an old man of about sixty sitting beside it smoking a pipe. Wishing to find out exactly where I had come, I approached him and asked him in halting English, 'Do you speak English?' 'Nein,' he replied arrogantly, in the tone of a man who had seen his nation beaten twice by the British but had never admitted defeat. Then, turning towards the boathouse, he shouted 'Inga', and as a young German girl appeared in the doorway he pointed at me in an ignominious way with the stem of his pipe.

'Aha,' I said. 'Can you help me?' 'I will try,' she said with a friendly smile. At the time, this girl appeared to me to be nothing more than a direction-finder in my efforts to discover a suitable place for an exercise. I did not notice her as a woman, or hardly even as a human being. She might well have been described in an Army pamphlet as a 'local inhabitant of an area' who 'will often prove of considerable value in orientating your position'.

Although she must have been of medium height, the impression that remains with me is of a heavily built girl whose figure radiated a considerable voluptuousness. Her legs were strong and her calves were thick and muscular. Nevertheless, she had a good waist and large, soft, feminine breasts that her dress contained with difficulty. Looking back on it her face, to English taste, would have appeared too full of expression and character. In fact, when

I showed my sister a photograph of her face she described her as looking like a tart!

It must have been the extreme sensuality of this girl, coupled with her forthright and completely uninhibited approach, that overcame my reserve and shyness. Very quickly we were discussing the beauty of the lake, the islands in its midst and the yachts that lay becalmed throughout its length.

You will understand that any girl that I had ever met before had been as unapproachable as my own shyness had been unconquerable and inbred. Having been educated at an English public school, my whole concept of the opposite sex was, to say the least, distorted. On this occasion, however, I was able to talk and joke with a girl quite freely – indeed, far more freely than my own sense of dignity allowed with my own male friends.

Returning to the camp that night I felt a different man. The feeling of incompleteness that had worried me earlier in the day was gone. As I drove into the camp I passed a group of the men's women who giggled and whispered to one another in an attempt to embarrass me.

My arrogance was, however, now complete, since added to the adolescent pomposity engendered by my rank I also felt an inherent superiority over the Jocks and their whores. Before, although I despised these women and was revolted by their activities, I had no girl of my own. Now I knew a clean, pleasant and wholly attractive German girl who in her looks and conversation was suited to a young officer.

That evening I ordered McDade, my batman, and three other men to inflate the rubber dinghy and to arrange for some sandwiches and a Thermos of tea to be ready in the morning. At lunchtime the next day they carried it down to the water for me, and, having placed it on the beach, they returned and sat on the hill.

At two o'clock Inga came to meet me as I had arranged, and together we pushed the boat into the lake and set off for a picnic. As I paddled away the four Jocks cheered, laughed and waved and, proud of my conquest, I waved back laughingly, understanding how envious they must have been of my good fortune.

After paddling slowly across the lake for an hour I suggested to Inga that we land on a small island and eat the tea that I had brought. She gaily agreed. There for hours I toyed with her, uncertain and hesitant in my actions until she, realising that she was in the hands of a completely inexperienced young man, took control and by suggestion and subtle innuendo indicated the parts of her body that gave her pleasure.

However, it was not until darkness came that I could contain my embarrassment sufficiently to explore her buxom body with anything bordering on military precision, and even then it would have been difficult to tell who was the more active partner or love's leader.

As the lesson progressed through the gathering darkness, my confidence increased and in the same way that an intangible bond grows up after two Englishmen have sat opposite each other in an otherwise empty railway carriage for four hours without speaking, conversation started and we began to learn about each other and the background to our lives.

'My father and mother were killed by the Russians,' Inga told me, 'when they conquered Berlin and something horrible happened to me. Now I live with my grandparents in Spandau, but they are very old.' 'Do you ever go out in the evening,' I asked, 'with any German boys?' 'There are very few German boys in Berlin,' said Inga. 'You speak such good English – I suppose you learned it at school?' 'Well, yes, a little, in fact all. And what about you? You are an English officer and so nice – my grandfather would hate my going out with an English officer. I like the English though, and especially the Scottish.' 'Do you know any of them?' 'Oh, only one or two…'

It must have been at about midnight that we reached the edge of the lake and I walked up the path past the camp with Inga and on through the trees for a mile to the main road where I kissed her goodbye. And as I wandered back through the darkness I felt weighed down by sympathy for her life and the terrible tragedies of her youth. Yet at the same time the knowledge that she had confided in me, had given herself to me, and had wept at the thought of one day leaving her, engendered in me a kind of humility that until that day I had lacked. I could no longer feel smug or arrogant because for the first time in my life I had understood and become part of someone other than myself.

Yet as I approached the camp my thoughts were rudely jerked back to the reality of my position and the responsibility that was mine with the men under my command. Sadly I reflected how great could be the benefits that 'my Jocks' might derive from friendship with such a girl instead of their incessant squalid serial acts of physical love in which they indulged with the half-human women of their acquaintance.

Wearily, as I reached my tent, I sank down upon my bed to find McDade faithfully awaiting my arrival with a mug of tea in his hand.

'Oh, well done, McDade,' I said. 'My goodness I'm thirsty. How did you guess how welcome this would be?' McDade just grinned and said, 'I just knew, sir. Oh, how did you find her? A bit of all right, I bet.' 'Yes – jolly good,' I said, quite startled. 'What do you mean?' 'Oh, only that we reckon Inga's the best bang in Berlin. Until tonight you were the only one in the platoon who hadn't bedded her. Goodnight, sir,' he said and disappeared.

The Scottish couple enjoyed my story. I retired to my bunk feeling much more cheerful.

49

The Fountainhead of Political Correctness

Quite the greatest pleasure of the cruise is that it is impossible to buy an English newspaper; my wife wants to keep a-breast (sic) of news back home – traffic gridlock, teenage sex, global warming, floods, juvenile courts, tanks at Heathrow, etc. – but no one here has heard of the British press, another mark of Viking wisdom.

However, on the sixth day – when the sheer tedium of the cruise is setting in – my wife arrives back from a jaunt around Honningsvag, a small harbour in the Arctic Circle, bearing a copy of Wednesday's *Guardian*; this liberal virus is spreading to the cleanest places. I am horrified.

'The *Guardian*,' I say. 'Do you want to disgrace me? Have you given no thought to my dignity and self-esteem? Suppose there is a spy from MI6 disguised as a Norwegian waiter, reporting back on all our contacts to the monstrous billion pound palace on the banks of the Thames [HQ of the Secret Intelligence Service – and financed by me while I was at the MOD]. If I am known to be a reader of the *Guardian*, I will never be able to shake off the spooks from counterintelligence and it will be noted in my "file".

'Worse still,' I continue, 'suppose there is a lurking female paparazzi disguised as a Norwegian chambermaid (cabin cleaner) with a hidden camera in her size 34FF (Jordan) bra, and she photographs me reading that liberal rag – and then the photograph is published in the *Daily Telegraph*; I shall be a leper in society. How can you pollute our cabin with such rubbish?' My wife replies, 'When you told me you were investigating modern Britain I thought you would be pleased to see the *Guardian*, the fountainhead of PC – political correctness. I bought the *Guardian* for your education.'

Indeed, when my wife leaves our cabin, out of curiosity I sneak a look at this newspaper, which I have never seen before. It seems to be devoted to advertisements for job seekers in the public sector: 'Do you want to be a social worker in Leeds?' 'Are you qualified to be a tea lady for a job centre in Camden?' I see the 'Judge Offer' – 'Hey, you! Wanna be a High Court judge, etc.' – mentioned on page 74. 'Are you fond of the countryside? If so, apply to be an Underground driver with London Transport.' 'The Cabinet Office is looking for an adviser to work on its plan for a more embracing, comprehensive, user-friendly and protective [nanny] state.' 'HM Treasury is seeking someone who is attracted to making a career as a lavatory hygiene supervisor for a nationwide chain of unisex public lavatories [OTPOTSS]' (see page 51).

I am really very interested because I am finding life difficult on a pensioner's fixed income – and there are all those well-paid jobs in the fastest-growing – indeed, the only growing – part of our economy, the public sector. My wife also goes banging on and on about the need to keep my brain active in retirement – and here it all is. But the problem is a substantial one: am I qualified for these arduous posts? I have gone through life as an amateur: an amateur soldier, amateur politician, amateur investment banker and amateur industrial chairman. I shall undoubtedly be asked to take a psychometric test, and I would have been unemployable if these tests had come in earlier.

The 'modernisers' have now brought in psychometric tests for aspiring Conservative parliamentary candidates, and they seem destined to produce exactly the kind of Tory MP that nobody wants. The strength of the Tory MP is that he is deeply unintelligent – and long may it remain so; we don't want a parliamentary party made up of clones of David Mellor. The Tory parliamentary party that I joined in 1966 consisted of Knights of the Shires, retired admirals, ex-wartime spooks and war heroes of every description. None of them could ever have passed an intelligence test; that was the great source of the Conservative Party's strength – when it won elections.

Modern, ill-educated youth, to whom I am addressing my journal, may not know that one of the Victorians most famous inventors was called Dr Crapper, the inventor of what they call the toilet. Dr Crapper, like the Victorians' generally, was very refined and he called the toilet a privy. It seems that the only qualification that I possess for the job is that I am a 'privy' councillor. Although Gordon Brown is advertising for a lavatory hygiene 'supervisor', as a 'privy' councillor I have already qualified on the first rung of this career ladder, so that one day I may rise to the dizzy heights of privy supervisor. It is worth a try. I do so very much want to join the public sector with its huge financial underpinning (taxes) when I have wasted so much of my life in the unfashionable, wealth-creating world of private business.

Having got the public sector job ads behind me, I read on and see a cross-section of *Guardian* opinion. I am appalled; it is a load of sanctimonious, patronising, politically correct 'nanny-knows-best' twaddle about the behaviour of British youth abroad. I have a high opinion of British youth. The paper contains a rabid attack on the leisure pursuits of my Viking cousins in places like Ibiza, Ayia Napa, Corfu, Faliraki, Mykonos and around various football grounds on the continent of Europe. These are the descendants of the men who – against overwhelming odds – won the Battle of Agincourt. If these fellow countrymen and women wish to follow the hereditary Viking pursuits of fighting, pillage and sex, would the *Guardian* prefer it if they did it in Cheltenham, Bournemouth and Belgravia? There is hope that our European partners will become so outraged at the behaviour of British youth that they will erect multilingual notices in all continental ports of entry:

EINGANG VERBOTEN
ENTRATA VIETATA
ENTRÉE INTERDIT
ΑΤΤΑΓΟΡΕΥΕΤΑΙ Η ΕΙΣΟΔΟΣ

Visas will be introduced for all Brits who cross the Channel and an integrated European Union will be fatally undermined. 'Once again Great Britain will have "saved" Europe from itself, etc., etc.' (© speech, Margaret Thatcher)

50

It's All Greek to Me

Since I am all at sea at present but still thinking about modern Britain I am reminded that in 1850 a Portuguese moneylender called Don Pacifico, who was born in Gibraltar and therefore had British nationality, had his house burnt down by a Greek mob in Athens. He lodged an outrageously exaggerated claim of £26,000 against the Greek government which, reasonably enough, refused to pay. Palmerston, in support of this British national, sent the British fleet to Athens with its guns trained on the Acropolis, ordered a blockage of Greek ports and seized all the Greek ships in the Port of Piraeus.

Palmerston spoke to the House of Commons as follows:

'A British subject, in whatever land he may be, shall feel confident that the watchful eye and the strong arm of England will protect him against injustice and wrong.'

Today the Saudi government arrests and tortures British subjects on forced confessions – and the supine Foreign

Office advises the released British subjects not to
complain; friendly British football supporters, provoked
by Turkish and German football hooligans, are execrated
in the politically correct British press and their passports
are confiscated; a band of perfectly ordinary and well-
behaved British citizens are arrested and charged for plane
spotting (spying) and the Foreign Office 'does its best to
help'. And so on.

Palmerston, in instant retaliation, would have thrown
Stelios (the founder) of easyJet into a rotting, damp jail for
inspecting his aeroplanes at Luton airport. Gordon Brown,
instead of dithering around for years, should have made all
the rich ship-owning Greeks pay their taxes like the rest of
us. But Oh No. The pusillanimous Foreign Office wants to
be friends to all foreigners, and especially to the Greeks, so
it plans to return 'The Marbles' to polluted Athens.

It is hard to judge which is more useless, the 'softly,
softly' British Foreign Office or the new maroon Euro-
passport which we are all forced to carry:

> *'A Euro subject in whatever land he may be shall feel
> confident that the watchful eye and the strong arm of
> President Prodi and Commissioner Patten will
> protect him against injustice and wrong.'*

Is it any wonder that young Brits take the first cheap flight
out of Stansted to escape Blair's Nanny State to relax in
Aya Nappa, Ibiza, Corfu and Rhodes where they make
intermittent attempts to follow the good example of Lord
Palmerston?

As part of my research into modern Britain and the younger Viking generation of England, I wonder why young people should want to go to Greece at all when they are likely to be arrested, thrown into jail and generally roughed up on beaches and in bars by Greek colonels. As I have already noted, all rich Greeks live tax free in Grosvenor Square and, apart from occasional visits in their yachts to remote islands in the Ionian Sea, they avoid their own country like the plague. Mr John Latsis, Prince Charles's yachting benefactor, lives in Geneva, Lord Taki of the *Spectator* lives in Gstaad, Alexander the Great came from Macedonia, Onassis was a Turk and lived in Monte Carlo.

So far as I am aware the only 'Greek' who even wanted to get back into that country is ex-King Constantine and he is a Dane, descended from the Schleswig-Holstein-Sonderburg-Glucksbergs. It's all Greek to me. As an ex-Dane myself I have thought of applying for his job. But the Greek government, advised by that famous image-maker Lord (Ding Dong) Bell – other client, the Conservative Party – has other proposals. Lord Bell is negotiating with the Foreign Office to offer Prince Andrew a job. He is of impeccable Greco-German ancestry and there is a strong move to get him off the golf course and away from British trade. Maybe I shall live long enough to see King Andrew and Queen Fergiana on the throne of Greece. This is not fanciful at all. The Greek throne was first offered to Queen Victoria's second son, Prince Alfred, in 1862, but the British government said 'No'. This time round the British government would say 'Yes' with alacrity, amidst much public rejoicing at the departure quay.

51

King John – The 'Fourth Way'

It must have been the Northern Lights that did it – and maybe all those thoughts about the throne of Greece. We were sailing on from Tromsö, the gateway to the Arctic, through wide fjords surrounded by snow-clad mountains. An announcement on the ship's Tannoy said that we could see the Northern Lights on the port side; so I left the cabin in my pyjamas and gazed at them for a time before returning to my bunk.

On my return I fell into a deep sleep and then had a vivid dream – or should I say a vision? I knew with 'certainty' that I was the lawful Viking heir to the throne of England!

My dream went like this: the Mountbatten-Windsors (their 'family' name) trace their descent principally from a continental usurper, Duke William of Normandy, who snatched the English crown from my Scandinavian ancestors in 1066. It was at the Battle of Stamford Bridge that Harald Hardrada, King of Norway, and his Viking army was defeated by Harold II of England (Hardrada had been promised the English throne by King Sweyn and King Harthacanute of England). Harold II marched his exhausted Saxon warriors south, after defeating the Viking host at Stamford Bridge, and immediately confronted William the Bastard of Normandy, to be in turn defeated by him, the Norman conqueror. The defeat of the Vikings at the Battle of Stamford Bridge in 1066 has been the cause of so many of our nation's troubles and of all the misfortunes that have befallen the Notts or the Canutes ever since. I knew it with certainty in my dream!

As I have already said, the name Nott is derived from the Danish name of Knott, Knut, Cnut, or Canute. When Canute, the son of Sweyn Forkbeard, King of Denmark and England, laid claim by right of conquest to the English throne, the Saxon Witan chose him as King of England in preference to the son of Ethelred.

The great King Canute, King of England, Denmark, Norway and the Hebrides, united the northern maritime nations into a great hegemony. He set out to reconcile the indigenous inhabitants with the new Viking arrivals into a single united people: the Anglo-Danish people of England thrived. Canute was truly the first King of the United Kingdom of England. Trade flourished in northern Europe and the Port of London became for the first time a great independent centre of power. Danish merchants became the leading citizens in London, as did my ancestor John Nott, Sheriff and Mayor of London in 1363. It was all very different from the Latin culture of France and from the history of Paris, the dwelling-place of the soft and pleasure-seeking kings of France.

While the Normans expropriated all the land owned by my Anglo-Danish forebears, the Danes, in contrast, did not indulge in a major land grab. England was rich in the tenth and eleventh centuries and the Danish King depended not on the later centralising power of the Normans but on a decentralised structure. The Vikings were independent-minded, freehanded and pleasure-loving, utterly different from the servitude demanded by the conquerors from Normandy who had absorbed the Latin feudal culture of the European continent. The Saxon Witan chose the ruler on a test of character and circumstance, not automatically on the basis of primogeniture. Just think how the kings and queens of England might have been different had not primogeniture and a fear of Catholicism inflicted us with the German-speaking Hanoverians and foreign-sounding Battenburgs, Saxe-Coburg-Gothas, Mecklenburg-Strelitzs and Schleswig-Holstein-Sonderburg-Gluckburgs. The Saxon Witan would hardly have elected the ghastly Hanoverians to the throne of England.

Princess Caroline of Brunswick, the vulgar and rejected wife of George IV, complained only a few weeks after her wedding that her husband's 'blackguard companions … were constantly drunk and filthy, sleeping and snoring in boots on the sofas'.

Princess Caroline was hardly an arbiter of taste and refinement but she captured something of the extravagant, coarse and licentious nature of her in-laws, particularly her husband's obnoxious brothers, the Royal Dukes of Kent (the father of Queen Victoria – although it was widely supposed that the elderly Duke was infertile and that Victoria was the illegitimate daughter of the German

Duchess of Kent and her Private Secretary, Sir John Conroy), Clarence (who became William IV – the very fertile father of ten illegitimate children by Mrs Jordan, the famous comic actress; he eventually lost the succession in what was humorously known as 'Hymen's War Terrific' to the Coburg Duchess of Kent and Sir John Conroy), York, Cumberland, Sussex and Cambridge. The Duke of Wellington said of them: 'My God! They are the damnedest millstone about the necks of any government that can be imagined. They have insulted – personally insulted – two-thirds of the gentlemen of England …'

In default of the descendants of Canute (the Notts) we would have been better served, as many Tories thought at the time, with the Catholic Stuarts (James III, 'the old Pretender', and his son, Bonnie Prince Charlie); but not for the first and last time the Whigs let us down by opting for the Hanoverian settlement.

Had Canute lived until sixty, I dreamed, instead of dying at the age of forty, his foresight and brilliance might have cemented a great Nordic empire astride the North Sea, with Scandinavia as one pillar and England as the other – a medieval EFTA, to use today's analogy. It might have changed the history of Europe. Instead, as a result of pure ill-luck, we were conquered by the Normans and suffered the servitude of French feudalism – centralising, authoritarian and bureaucratic, as beautifully exemplified today by the European Union.

It was not until four hundred years later that the English recovered their sense of freedom and independence which led them to go out and build an empire, just as their Viking ancestors had done before them. Thus we lost four hundred years of opportunity under the yoke of European influence – and now many educated Englishmen want to hand us back to Europe and make us vassals of the Holy Roman Empire in Brussels.

So, in my dream, I pondered what I could do about it. With the genes of Halvdan the Black (I am fair-skinned), Harald Fairhair (I am bald), Harald Bluetooth (my dentist is at 90 Harley Street) and Erik Bloodaxe (Lieutenant Nott, 2nd Gurkha Rifles, retired) I have a duty to put things right before the European Union destroys us all. And here my vision gave me guidance. I have nothing but admiration for our beloved Queen – she has been an outstanding monarch – but her right to the throne of England is much less clear than mine. There is little doubt that the senior line comes down from Canute direct to me, but I need, of course, to prove it.

First, my vision directed me to attempt to claim the throne of England by legal means. On my return from my Viking homeland I shall seek out the Earl Marshal at the College of Arms and slap my pedigree in front of him. I am not expecting him to be particularly friendly or accommo-dating. The Earl Marshal is of Norman descent, and he will undoubtedly feel threatened if a Danish king is re-estab-lished on the English throne. He may lose his job as well as his fancy clothes. He has thrown in his lot with the Mountbatten-Windsors and I am not expecting him to switch his allegiance to the Notts.

If this fails, what then? Having sailed the fjords of Norway and seen my distant cousins on their farms, and actually feeling the blood of Erik Bloodaxe surging through my veins, I can hardly give up the struggle, and here I will show the cunning of the Mountbatten-Windsors. After all, you do not cling to the throne of England for a thousand years without being devious and manipulative on occasions.

My next move is as follows. The bones of Canute are in a casket in Winchester Cathedral. I shall give my blood so that my DNA can then be compared with the bones of my ancestor. No one can contradict that Canute had an earlier claim to the throne of England than William of Normandy, so I shall then request that a member of the royal family cooperate. Prince Edward, inaptly named the Earl of Wessex, has some Scottish blood and may, for all I know, have a tiny drop of English blood as well; and for publicity (see Court Circular below) he might well be prepared to give some help. His sample we can then compare with mine. I can see it now:

Court Circular
Buckingham Palace

Prince Edward, Earl of Wessex, today gave blood (blue) to the Rt Hon Sir John Nott whose blood (red) has also been transferred by the Royal Train to the King Edward VII Hospital for tests.

If my DNA is closer to Canute's than this sprig from the Norman line – hey presto! I have proved my claim.

But I have to protect myself against the dirty tricks department – the Mountbatten-Windsor spin machine.

Leaving the splendid efforts of Sir John Conroy on one side we all suspect that George III, when Prince of Wales and before the passing of the Royal Marriages Act in 1772, went through a legal first marriage on 17 April 1759 to Hannah Lightfoot, the daughter of a Wapping shoemaker, and that she produced children. If I have the greatest claim to the throne of England, clearly the descendants of George III and Hannah Lightfoot, let alone Sir John Conroy, have the next greatest claim. But every effort of historians and other serious-minded scholars to examine the records of George III's private life, which are in the archives in Windsor, has been frustrated. Of course, if George III had legitimate heirs in advance of his bigamous marriage to Queen Charlotte, the Mountbatten-Windsors' claim is doubly unsound. I cannot therefore expect that the confidential family records in Windsor proving the pedigree of the Mountbatten-Windsors will be made available to me.

If I am obstructed in my claim, I have to contemplate the fourth and final route, namely violence. With Erik Bloodaxe and Harald Hardrada in my pedigree, I have inherited a concealed talent for violence. But it would be unwise to reveal my strategy. As a former Defence Secretary, it is obvious that you do not reveal your battle plans in advance.

If successful by any of these routes, I would of course re-establish the divine right of kings. There would be no wishy-washy constitutional settlement. Things would change dramatically. I would immediately withdraw from the European Union, dissolve Parliament and restore the Saxon Witan, who would be required to agree that character and circumstance confirmed my right to the Crown. This done, I would send the well-meaning Mr Blair into exile in Brussels, put Gordon Brown the tax-gatherer in the Tower of London, where he would not last long, and would then appoint an all-female celebrity privy council in honour of Canute's English concubine, who produced several successors. I am one of them.

The appointment of a group of celebrities as a female privy council should ensure that the female population of England supports me and helps to make me a popular king. I have not yet made a final choice of members, but my privy council might consist of Edwina Currie, Cherie Blair, Ann Widdecombe, Liz Hurley, Naomi Campbell, Carole Caplin (uninvited) and Posh Spice – a distinguished and eclectic bunch for sure.

Having shown my appreciation of womankind, and having got the female population of England on my side, I would then build up support among the dispossessed, by this time to include the homeless and all former Tory Members of Parliament. Having studied the dissolution of the monasteries, I would take over all the cultural institutions of the country, including the Royal Opera House, the BBC, the National Theatre, the Festival Hall, all the Tates and the University of Oxford and throw out the subsidised élite who run these places. I would then equip all these institutions as dosshouses for the dispossessed under the management of the Salvation Army. In this way, the majority of the population, freed from the parasitic world of businessmen and the cultural élite, would feel that their personal interests and future were closely linked with mine.

King John II (me) supported by two seated 'Privy' Councillors.

All former Liberal and New Labour MPs, including Heseltine, Howe, Hurd, Heath, Patten, Britten, Clarke and other Tory Europhiles of the anti-English tendency, would be deported to join Blair in Brussels.

I wake up with a start. The boat is docking at Kirkenes near the Russian border. Was this a dream? It all seemed so necessary, accurate and real. But there is a problem: I don't want to be King of England one little bit. What is a throne? A bit of wood covered in velvet. Frederick the Great described his crown as only a hat that let in water. And Shakespeare said, 'what hath Kings that privates have not too – save ceremony?'

It would be demeaning to live a life of pretence and servitude to the British people, continually subject to the lies and inventions of the British press; and worst of all, I would be expected to dress up in fancy clothes and spend huge sums of other people's money keeping up appearances. I abhor extravagance and ceremonial, as my journal makes all too clear. No – it's not my scene at all.

Thus ends my Norwegian cruise – and a great Viking experience.

52

'Eheu fugaces ... labuntur anni'
('Alas, the fleeting years slip away' – Horace)

On the flight back from Kirkenes to Oslo I try to sleep. Suddenly the plane is swaying everywhere and turns from right to left; then, without any warning it flies upside down. I realise that I have vertigo and this time it is really bad. The problem must be my very heavy cold, caused by gazing at the Northern Lights in my pyjamas.

I had noticed when we climbed on to the plane that there was a leggy and very lovely blonde air hostess and, as I put my head between my legs, sweating profusely – so much so that my shirt is sopping wet – this blonde beauty comes rushing up to me – first with water, then with orange juice, then with ice packed in a flannel to cool me down, then with two plastic glasses into which she has inserted hot rags, which she says I must put over my ears to create a vacuum. I explain that I have suffered from vertigo before.

Then the Norwegian air hostess rushes up to me again, as if she has an exceptional crisis on her hands in the midst of her mundane duties, and she gives me some nasal sprays by Merck. I stuff them up my nose and squeeze. This dish leans all over me and I look sideways up to her and say, three inches from her face, 'I'm rather enjoying this'. She smiles. Oh dear. Why am I seventy? Here today, gone tomorrow.

Epilogue

And now I am done. I have been around London and out of London. I have tea-danced with widows in Bromley, Battersea and Hammersmith, all to no avail as it turned out. I have swum with sharks at the Savoy. Julian Dobson's Bridge Club was educational; so, in its way, was Spearmint Rhino, where in a single lunchtime I thought I had made a friend for life in Pam. Yes, she was certainly educational. I have witnessed the vibrant cultures in the markets of south, west and east London; I have met a man called Mr Wonderful and been introduced, if not personally, to Commander Cressida Dick, although I feel I know her well. I have discovered the pleasures and perils of the number 19 and 22 buses, and, with any luck, set back the surveys of political focus groups a few years. I have seen the future for my white van, and it looks beautiful.

At the end of this momentous and enlivening survey, I am sitting at home with my wife and we are having a candlelit dinner to celebrate the final entry. My wife knows that the salacious content of my journal is mostly in the fervid imagination of a seventy-year-old man in the grip of his belated menopause. She is indulgent and by now rather bored with my reminiscences of misdemeanours. I look across the table and consider myself to be very lucky to have married such a remarkable, interesting and generous woman.

Seeing her in the glow of the candlelight brings back to me that sense of excitement, that fascination bordering on obsession, that captivated me when I first set eyes on her forty-five years ago in Cambridge. 'I am going to marry you,' I told her, at her own engagement party to another undergraduate. Since then, my behaviour has often been equally impulsive and regrettable, but she has stuck with me through thick and thin, 'for better or for worse'.

My wife asks me, now that all is said and done, how I judge what I have seen; if the country has changed dramatically during the years in which I was 'trapped' by my career.

I reply that the elderly must not become old Grundys, deploring the modern world, saying that the country is not what it was. It never has been. The world goes on its own way whether the old and critical approve of it or not. There are problems – too many divorces, single mothers, more crime, in many respects *less* leisure. But there is good in it as well. Men are better fathers than they were; there is much greater prosperity; there is the breakdown of class distinctions. There is certainly poverty, an underclass, but the so-called working class has moved up seamlessly into the middle class. It is no longer a bucket-and-spade holiday in Blackpool or Clacton, but a twice-yearly excursion on easyJet or Ryanair to Spain – or even a weekend in Ibiza for the young. If you want to witness this, go to Gatwick Airport at any time – that's the place to see the England of today.

My wife has her own opinion. She says that life changed in the 1960s; the pill – actually, where my journal begins – made women more free, more promiscuous if you like. There was no longer the same fear of pregnancy. Education became more widespread; women started to go to university in greater numbers. Educated women were no longer prepared to be just housewives and the chattels of their husbands; they started to make decisions about their own lives, sexually and materially. So much of this was positive but it had its negative consequences, especially for children.

But my wife and I agree. The most fundamental change in our lifetime has been the emancipation of women. For good or ill, it has changed our society – much more so than immigration. The only alternative in earlier times to the loneliness of spinsterhood was marriage and the slavery of child-rearing; it is now a career. Marriage and child-rearing bring huge rewards but it is at the expense of personal independence. Now women have a choice which they did not have when I was born. The pill – as well as the morning-after pill – has brought about, indirectly maybe, the most dramatic change in my lifetime. More so than the Second World War, and the explosion of technology and knowledge, of which effective contraception is a major consequence.

There has been no such change for men. Young men have always been a problem. Nothing much has changed for them except that we have no wars to speak of, no colonies to occupy their energies. There has always been crime and disorder on the streets but nowadays there are too few police, there is no press gang, no National Service, less participatory as opposed to spectator sport. In the sports pubs you notice that young men have lost a lot of their respect for women – they are frightened of marrying because the women have become more like the men, and have lost so much of the femininity which was their principal attraction to the opposite sex. The women decide when they want to have sex, when they have children, when they pursue a career. The men are muted; there is less scope for them to be protective males. If we cannot put the clock back and de-emancipate women, we could at least try harder to do something for our young men.

It is hardly surprising that today's heroes are not Albert Schweitzer, Mother Teresa or the astonishing men whose feats of bravery and endurance we read about in today's obituaries, but celebrities like David Beckham. I think Beckham is a rather admirable young man, but, although in one sense he wears his success quite modestly, nobody has done more to encourage the false impression that achievement is measured today by the size of a designer wardrobe and by the frequency with which a picture appears in newspaper gossip columns or weekly glossies.

If the spiritual appears to have been usurped by the temporal, of all my experiences and adventures, the one that had the greatest impact on me was my evening visit to Holy Trinity, Brompton. I could see that hundreds of young people in the congregation were seeking some meaning to life ('the peace of God that passeth all understanding'), something more permanent than money and celebrity status. I suspect that most of our new citizens, as represented by those I encountered in Tooting, Hammersmith and Upton Park, have found that meaning. But although I was impressed by what I saw at Holy Trinity, I am unlikely to become a convert to charismatic evangelism as I tend to believe that Jesus was a great prophet – and only the Son of God in the sense that we are all children of God. As I grow older I am not anticipating immortality – lying in the bosom of thirty virgins (who would all be quarrelling among themselves) – but I think that in so far as we gain immortality we live on in the genes of our descendants; King Canute still survives through me! I am, however, attracted to the Buddhist concept of the transmigration of souls; I expect to return as a worm rather than as a Brahmin or a minor royal.

I wish I could be anything other than offended by the modern Church of England. But, like modern politics, it has debased itself to the focus group. It is concerned with accommodating modern life rather than confronting its obvious evils. It is obsessed with marketing for customers rather than preaching principle. What used to attract me to the Church was its sense of comradeship and its historical continuity, the beauties of the Anglican tradition. But our trendy priests of today are engaged in destroying the tradition and language of the Church. They might as well abandon them openly, like Holy Trinity, Brompton, and base their appeal on religious karaoke – scripture and emotion.

But if I take Islam, the religions of the East, the smells, bells and rituals of Catholicism, charismatic evangelism and the Anglicanism of my youth, which of them will protect my poor soul when it reappears in the entrails of a worm? The answer has been obvious throughout my Norwegian cruise – my personal road to Damascus – if only I had recognised it earlier.

My protector will be the Viking god Thor, the son of Odin, who gave his name, via the Romans, to 'Thursday'.

He was the foremost of the gods to the common man. The revelation came to me in a flash of lightning as I completed my writing on a Thursday. Thor is the god of thunder; of agriculture, farmers and free men – all the things that mean most to me. As the god of thunder he travels above the clouds in a carriage drawn by two goats. He is also the god of fertility and he drinks a lot of *mjod* (beer). He is righteous and has a violent temper. I am much attracted to him. According to Viking mythology, 'in the time of Ragnarok [the end of the world] Thor dies in a battle with a gigantic worm called Midgard'. Maybe one small Viking worm will return to the bosom of another.

People will say that this is pure paganism but I say to my Christian friends, 'step back and ask yourselves: is there nothing pagan in the rituals and practices of the Christian Church?' Belief in Thor flourished alongside Christianity long after the conversion of my Viking ancestors, a thousand years ago. If it was good enough for the warriors at Stamford Bridge, it is good enough for me.